FHM PRESENTS
THE BEST OF BAR ROOM
JOKES 2

This is a Carlton Book
Copyright © 2003 Emap Elan Network

This edition published 2003 by Carlton Books Limited
20 Mortimer Street
London W1T 3JW

A CIP catalogue record for this book is available from the British Library.

ISBN 1 84442 971 7

Illustrations: Nishant Choksi, David Semple
Design: Paul Rider

Thanks to FHM's readers for all their jokes

Printed and bound in Great Britain

FHM PRESENTS
THE BEST OF BAR ROOM
JOKES 2

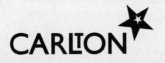

What's the difference...

...between a rebellious chicken and a randy solicitor? One clucks defiance...

The Australian virgin

A rich young heiress decided one day she was fed up with all the men she'd ever slept with, as none of them had been a virgin. For once she wanted to bed a man who'd never had sex with anyone in their entire life, so she summoned her flunkies and told them to find her a virgin.

With money no object, her staff searched the planet, finally locating a young man from the Australian outback. Flown back to the UK, the young Aussie was bathed and scrubbed, before finally being allowed into the heiress's bedroom. But when he walked in he ignored the beautiful young woman lying on the bed; instead he put his weight behind the wardrobe and shunted it into the hallway, then rolled up the rug and tore down the curtains. "What are you doing?" the woman asked, dumbfounded. "It's true, I've never screwed a woman before," replied the Aussie. "But if it's anything like screwing a kangaroo, I'll be needing plenty of room."

The dozy parishioner

A woman who is constantly embarrassed by her husband falling asleep in church goes to the priest to ask for help. The priest says, "Look love, if he falls asleep again, poke him with this hat pin. I'll nod to you as a signal if I see him dropping off." The woman agrees to the plan. So Sunday rolls around and sure enough, good old Mr Jones nods off again. The priest notices and asks, "Who is our saviour?" then nods to Mrs Jones. She pokes her husband and he wakes up and shouts, "Jesus Christ!"

The priest, pretending to be impressed, says, "Very good!"

A full three minutes later, Mr Jones is asleep again. The priest again notices and asks, "What is the name of Jesus's father?" before nodding at Mrs Jones.

She pokes her husband, who screams, "GOD!" at the top of his lungs. The priest again congratulates Mr Jones on his alertness and continues preaching. However, during the sermon, he begins nodding enthusiastically, which Mrs Jones mistakes for a poking signal. The priest then says, "And what did Eve say to Adam after she gave him his 99th child?" Mistakenly Mrs Jones pokes her husband, who shouts, "If you poke that damn thing

A man walks into a bar...

...holding a newt. "A pint of lager for me," he says, "and a glass of cola for my pet, Tiny."
The bartender frowns at the man, puzzled. "Of all things, why d'you call him Tiny?" he asks.
"Well," says the man. "He is my newt."

Q: WHAT DO YOU CALL A LESBIAN WITH THICK FINGERS?

into me one more time, I'll snap it in half and shove it up your arse!"

On the house

A barman walks over to a waiting customer and asks, "What'll it be, sir?"

"Make it a large Scotch," says the man.

"No problem," replies the bartender, handing over the drink. "That'll be £4.80."

"Actually," says the man, "I don't owe you anything." Overhearing the comment, a lawyer sat nearby wanders over. "You know, he's got you there," he explains to the barman. "In the original offer – which constitutes a binding contract upon acceptance – there was no stipulation of remuneration."

The bartender is unimpressed, but gives in. "Okay, you beat me this time… but don't let me catch either of you in here again."

The following day, the same man strolls into the bar. "What the hell are you doing?" shouts the barman, "I thought I told you not to come back?"

"I think you've mistaken me for someone else," replies the man, somewhat bewildered, "I've never been here before in my life."

"My apologies… but it's uncanny," explains the barman, "you must have a double."

"Well," says the man, "if you insist – make it a large Scotch."

How pies are made

A young man and his naive girlfriend were taking a leisurely stroll through the countryside when they happened across a huge bull shagging a cow. "What are they doing?" asked the young woman.

The man, not knowing what to say, replied, "They're making pies, my sweet." They carried on walking, the girl seeming satisfied with the answer. A few miles further on they stumbled across a great big ram shagging a small sheep. "And what are they doing?" asked the young woman.

To this the man replied, "They too are making pies." Again they carried on, and as they walked the man spotted a deserted barn. All this rambling had made him incredibly randy and, turning to his girlfriend, he enquired as to whether she would like to "make pies".

"Okay," she replied, and they disappeared into the barn, where the man shagged his girlfriend for dear life. Having finished, they carried on walking back to town. After a while the girl turned to the man and said, "I think the pies are done."

The man was confused. "Why's that, dear?"

"Because the gravy has just run down my leg."

> **What do you call…**
> **…a Scouser in a white shell suit?**
> ***The bride.***

What do you get...
...if you cross an agnostic, an insomniac and a dyslexic?
A man who lies awake at night, wondering if there really is a dog.

The novelty soap dispenser

Two priests are off to the showers late one night. They undress and step into the cubicles, before they realise there's no soap. Father John says he has soap in his room and goes to get it, not bothering to dress. He grabs two bars of soap and heads back to the showers, but is only halfway down the hall when he sees three nuns heading his way. Having no place to hide he stands against the wall and freezes like he's a statue.

The nuns stop and comment on how lifelike he looks. The first nun suddenly reaches out and pulls his dick. Startled, he drops a bar of soap. "Oh look," says the second nun, "a soap dispenser!"

To test her theory the second nun also pulls his dick and sure enough he drops the second bar of soap. The third nun then pulls, once, twice, three times, but still nothing happens. So she tries once more, and delightedly yells, "Look – hand cream!"

The mechanic's confession

A motor mechanic was working late alone in the garage and was under a car when some brake fluid dripped into his mouth. "Wow!" he said to himself. "This stuff doesn't taste too bad."

The next day he told his buddy about supping on the fluid. "It's not bad," he said. "Got a bit of a kick to it. Think I'll have a bit more today." His friend was a little concerned but didn't say anything.

The following day the mechanic confessed to drinking a cupful of brake fluid. "Great stuff! Think I'll have some more today." And so he did.

A week later the mechanic was up to a bottle a day, and his friend was now really worried. "Brake fluid's poisonous," he told his pal. "You'd better lay off the stuff."

"Hey, no problem," the mechanic replied. "I can stop any time."

What's the difference...
...between Gary Lineker and an Essex girl?
Gary Lineker's never scored more than four times in 90 minutes.

Q: WHAT'S LONG, THIN AND SMELLS OF PISS?

The dirty ducks

Two ducks check into a hotel for a dirty weekend. They can't wait to get up to their room, but then discover they've forgotten the condoms. "No problem," quacks the drake, "I'll just call down to room service and get them to bring a johnny up."

A few minutes later, room service is knocking at the door. The male duck waddles over, takes the condom and tips the lad. "Sir," asks the flunky, "should I put that on your bill?"

"Christ, no!" quacks the duck, startled. "What do you think I am, some kind of pervert?"

Death by chocolate

A policeman is pounding the beat when he gets an urgent message on his radio telling him a dead body has been found in an ice-cream van, just down the road. He rushes to the scene, where he discovers the body: it's a man with chocolate flakes up each nostril, raspberry sauce all over his head and covered from head to toe in hundreds and thousands. A puzzled onlooker asks the policeman what he thinks has happened.

"Looks like he topped himself," says the copper.

Man juice misdirected

There were two sperm swimming in a pink wonderland. One said to the other, "How far are we from the uterus?"

The other replies, "Ages, mate. We've only just passed the tonsils."

Beadle's about

Jeremy Beadle has gone on a secretarial course. He hopes it will improve his shorthand.

PENSIONERS DOING THE CONGA.

Snow joke

Why are women such poor skiers? There's not much snow between the bedroom and kitchen.

Calling all cars

Scotland Yard are having a crackdown on Viagra smugglers. Police are reported to be looking for 20 hardened criminals.

The archbishop's lunch

A vicar is walking along the riverbank, when he sees Frank loading his rod and tackle into his boat. "Fancy fishing, Vicar?" calls Frank.

"I can't today – I've got the archbishop coming to lunch," explains the vicar.

"Oh go on, just for an hour," cajoles Frank.

"All right then, but just for a short while." So the vicar and Frank push off and start fishing. Within minutes, Frank's got a massive bite and he spends the next half hour wrestling a huge fish aboard. "Look at the size of that fucker!" says Frank when the monster finally lies defeated on the floor of the boat.

"Frank," tuts the vicar, "it really is a prize specimen but the use of such language is unforgivable."

"You don't understand, Vicar," replies Frank, thinking fast. "This fish really is called a Fucker. Er... why don't you take it home for the archbishop's lunch?"

"Why thank you," says the man of God, "I'll clean it up and head home now." Back at the vicarage, the churchman plonks the fish on the table. "Look at the size of this Fucker!" he says to his housekeeper. She's shocked. "A fine fish it is but I can't believe you would use such language in the vicarage!" The vicar explains how that's the name of the fish so, slightly happier, she goes into the kitchen to start cooking. Soon the archbishop arrives, and sits down to lunch with the vicar. In comes the housekeeper with the cooked fish.

"Look at the size of this, archbishop," she says. "Frank caught the Fucker, the vicar cleaned the Fucker up and I cooked the Fucker for your lunch!" The archbishop beams, takes off his shoes, puts up his feet and starts to roll a joint. "You know," he says, "you bastards are all right."

Q: WHY WAS THE BLONDE SACKED FROM THE SPERM BANK?

What's the difference...
...between an oral thermometer and a rectal thermometer?
The taste.

What you can get for a tenner

A man is walking down the street when he notices that a brothel has opened up, so he decides to go in. As soon as he enters, the madam sidles up to him. He explains that he's extremely horny but because he didn't realise the knocking shop had opened he only has five quid with him.

She snatches the money from his hand and promises that she has the solution to his problem. Then she leads him down a hall and into a small room. Expecting to find a woman waiting there, the man can see only a chicken, clucking and pecking at the floor. He figures he was ripped off, so he paces around the room in frustration – but when his wood won't go down he decides to make love to the chicken, chasing the bird around the room before finally catching it.

Perhaps it is the thrill of the chase, but the sex is *amazing*. Unsurprisingly, the man returns to the brothel a week later, this time with a tenner in his pocket. He explains to the madam that he enjoyed himself so much before that he'd like to double his pleasure. Once again the madam grabs his money and leads him down another hallway and into a room, where a group of people are sitting around, staring through a window. He joins them and gazes in amazement at the sight of a couple at it like rabbits on the other side of what appears to be a two-way mirror.

Obviously the love-makers can't see the audience, which the man finds incredibly arousing. He turns to the bloke next to him and exclaims: "This is the most amazing thing I've ever seen in my life!"

The man responds, "That's nothing. You should have been here last week – we watched some sicko have it off with a chicken."

A man walks into a bar...

...and orders 12 shots of whisky. The bartender lines up a dozen shot glasses on the bar and fills them with Scotch. Quickly the man downs one after the other, until he's finished all 12.

"Well," says the bartender, "what are you celebrating?"

"My first blow job," says the man.

"In that case," says the bartender, smiling, "let me buy you one more!"

"No thanks," replies the man. "If 12 won't get the taste out of my mouth, nothing will."

A: SHE WAS CAUGHT DRINKING ON THE JOB.

The whistling salesman

One day a farmer caught a travelling salesman making love to his youngest daughter. "You son of a bitch!" he yelled, as he shot the amorous rep in the groin with a 12-gauge shotgun. The screaming salesman quickly took off for town to find a doctor. He found one, but the physician took one look at the man's dick and told him that nothing could be done for him. "Please do something," begged the salesman. "I'm a rich man and can pay you whatever you ask."

"Sorry, son," said the doctor. "It's beyond my ability. However, there's a man across the street who might be able to help."

"Is he a specialist?" gasped the salesman.

"No," said the doctor, "he's a piccolo player. He'll teach you how to hold your dick without pissing in your face."

Cheeky lad

A mother and her young son are having a bath together one night, when the son points in between his ma's legs and asks, "Mum, what's that?"

His mum replies, "Oh… that's where, er, God hit me with an axe."

"That was a good shot," her son replies. "Right in the cunt."

Tough trucker

After three weeks on the road, a trucker pulls in at a local brothel and bangs $500 on the counter. "Listen, lady," he says to the madam, "I want a really tough, overcooked steak and the ugliest woman you've got."

"What's your problem?" cries the madam. "For that sort of money I could give you a five-course, cordon bleu meal and the most beautiful girl in the place for the night."

The trucker glowers at her. "Listen, sweetheart," he snarls, "I'm not feeling horny, I'm feeling homesick."

Not a pretty sight

A man strolls into a lingerie shop and asks the assistant: "Do you have a see-through negligée, size 46-48-52?" The assistant looks bewildered. "What the hell would you want to see through that for?"

Woof!

Three heavily pregnant women meet on a maternity ward. The first woman says, "I was on my back during conception, so I'm going to have a girl."

The second one says, "Well, I was riding on top at conception, so I'm going to have a boy."

The third one looks horrified. "Oh shit," she says. "I'm going to have puppies!"

What do you call…
…a fanny on top of a fanny on top of a fanny on top of a fanny?
A block of flaps.

Q: WHAT DID DONALD DUCK SAY TO THE PROSTITUTE?

You get what you pay for

Eager to earn herself a little extra income, a blonde girl decided to hire herself out as a handyman-type and began canvassing a wealthy neighbourhood. The owner of a lavish mansion soon agreed to use her. "You could paint my porch – how much do you charge?" he asked.

The girl thought for a moment: "How about £50?"

The man duly agreed and informed his new employee that the paint and ladders she'd need were in the garage, then left her to get on with it. An uncomfortably short time later, the doorbell rang. "I've finished!" beamed the blonde girl proudly, "that'll be £50, please!"

"You've finished already?" asked the man, astounded by the girl's efficiency. "Of course," answered the blonde, "I even gave it two coats, just to be sure!" Impressed, the man handed her a crisp £50 note.

"Oh, and by the way, silly," the blonde added, "that's not a Porsche, it's a Ferrari."

Passion ignited!

Desperate to rekindle the spark in his marriage, a man returns home from work, finds his wife asleep in bed and plans a surprise. In he jumps, diving under the covers and pleasuring his lady with the most energetic oral sex he's ever given. After a few minutes of squirming, slurping and moaning, her body spasms with ecstasy and she enjoys an incredible climax.

Satisfied with his effort, the man goes to brush his teeth in the bathroom. In he goes… and there before him? His wife shaving her legs. "What the fuck are you doing in here?" he screams. "Shh…" she replies, pointing to the bed, "you'll wake your mother!"

A. PUT IT ON MY BILL.

What's the difference...
...between an egg and a wank?
You can beat an egg.

He never forgets

In his last days on Earth, Bob Hope accepts an invitation to go on _Surprise, Surprise_, where he brags to Cilla that, despite his 97 years of age, he could still have sex three times a night. After the show, Cilla wanders over. "Look Bob," she purrs, "I hope I'm not being too forward, but I'd love to have sex with an older man."

Smiling, the pair go back to her place and have great sex. Afterwards, Bob turns to the Liverpudlian loudhailer. "If you think that was good," he grins, "let me sleep for half an hour, and we'll do it again. But while I'm sleeping, hold my testicles in your left hand and my penis in your right hand."

Perplexed, Cilla nevertheless agrees – and after 30 minutes' kip Bob wakes up and, again, makes love like an athletic 25-year-old. As before, Bob then turns to the Mersey motormouth. "Cilla, that was wonderful," he smiles. "But if you let me sleep for an hour – again while holding my genitals – we can have the best sex yet." But Cilla is curious. "Bob, tell me," she asks. "Does my holding your testicles in my left hand and your penis in my right stimulate you while you're sleeping?"

Bob shakes his head. "No," he replies, "it's just that the last time I slept with a Scouser, she stole my wallet."

What's in a name?

A Native American boy asks his father, "How did you pick names for us kids, Pop?" "Well," the chief replies, "when your older brother was born, the first thing I saw when I came out of the teepee was an eagle soaring high in the sky. So I named him Flying Eagle. And when your little sister was born, the first thing I saw was a deer running away, so I named her Running Deer. Why do you ask, Fucking Dog?"

Suicide blonde

A blonde suspects her husband of fooling around. She follows him to his girlfriend's house one day, busts open the door and puts the gun to her own head.

The husband pipes up, "Honey! Don't do this!" "Shut up!" she says. "You're next."

What's the best way...
...to remember your wife's birthday?
Forget it once.

First things first

A man goes to see the doctor about a truly wretched gas problem. "Doc," he says nervously, "I'm suffering from this weird ailment in which I fart every few minutes. They sound like bloody thunderclaps! They don't seem to smell at all, but it's really embarrassing when I've got company."

Right on cue, the afflicted man emits a horrifyingly loud anal detonation, which almost blows him off his seat.

"Well," the doctor says, "I'll prescribe some pills for you. Take them every two hours and see me at the end of the week."

One week passes and the guy storms back into the surgery. "You bastard!" he screams. "Not only am I still passing gas, but now they smell as if something crawled up my arse and died!"

The doctor smiles. "Excellent. Now that you've got your sense of smell back, let's work on that farting problem."

The deaf bear

It's spring, and baby bear staggers out of his cave. His knees are wobbling, paws shaking – he's a wreck, all skin and bones with big circles under his eyes.

"Junior!" his mother says. "Did you hibernate all winter like you were supposed to?"

"Hibernate?" he says. "I thought you said masturbate!"

Dead or alive

A primary school pupil tells his teacher that he's just found a cat at the side of the road. "It's dead," he reveals.

"How do you know it's dead?" asks the teacher.

"Easy," says the child, "because I pissed in its ear and it didn't move."

"You did what?!" the teacher shouts.

"You know," explained the boy, "I leant over, went 'Pssst!' and it didn't move."

Which service…?

A Glaswegian woman dials 999 and requests an ambulance, telling the operator that she is pregnant.

"Madam, you can't have an ambulance simply because you're pregnant," explains the operator. "This line is for emergencies only."

"Och, ah know," says the woman, "but ma waaters have broke!"

"Oh – that's a different matter," says the operator. "Where are you ringing from?"

"Christ," the woman replies, "from ma fanny tae ma feet."

How the other half live

A rich man and his wife are being served dinner by their chef. "You know, dear," says the man, looking up from his soup, "if you could cook, we could fire the chef."

"That's true, darling," the wife responds. "And if you could fuck, we could fire the chauffeur."

What's the difference…
…between Twiggy and a fake American dollar?
One's a phoney buck…

> ## Why do men name their dicks?
> *Because they don't want a total stranger making 90 per cent of their decisions.*

A sweet story

Smartie and Polo are enjoying a quiet drink in a bar when the doors open and in walks Humbug. "Oh shit," mutters Polo, diving underneath the table. "What are you doing?" asks Smartie. "Humbug always slaps me around whenever I see him, so I'm hiding," explains Polo. "You should stand up to him," says Smartie. "He'll respect you if you do." As predicted, Humbug walks straight over and gives the mint a smack. "Piss off you stripy twat, or I'll knock your glazing off!" snarls Polo. "Oh, right…" says Humbug. "Sorry mate, I'll leave it." Next night, Polo and Smartie are once again sitting in the bar, when Humbug walks in with his friend, Tune. "Oh shit," says Smartie, diving for the floor. "What are you doing?" asks Polo. "I know I told you to stand up to bullies, but Humbug's with Tune!" hisses Smartie from under the table. "So?" says Polo. "He's fucking menthol!" says Smartie.

The lezzer's exam

A lesbian goes to see her GP for her annual check-up. The doc does an internal and says, "My, you're looking pretty clean these days." "I should be," the lesbian replies. "I have a woman in three times a week."

The blonde's audition

Hoping for a part in a seedy sex show, a stunning blonde presents herself at an agent's office. "What do you do, honey?" the agent asks. "I play the harmonica with my fanny," she replies. The blonde then gives a demonstration of her special talent. "Fantastic," enthuses the agent, reaching for the telephone. "Keep on playing while I phone the producer of the show." Holding the phone out towards the performing blonde, the agent gets the producer on the line. "What do you think of this?" he shouts over the performance. "What the hell are you playing at?" bellows the producer. "You drag me out of bed just to hear some cunt play the harmonica?"

> ## What do you call...
> *...an Australian with a sheep under one arm and a goat under the other? Bisexual.*

Q: WHAT DO YOU SAY TO AN OUT-OF-WORK ACTOR?

Unlucky purchase

A young man walks into a chemist's and asks for a pack of condoms. "Hot date?" says the pharmacist. "You betcha," says the horny youngster. "My new girl and I are driving to the lake tonight – gonna steam up some windows!" When he goes to pick up his date, she invites him in to meet the parents. After the usual stilted pleased to meet yous, the young man tells his date, "Hey – instead of going out tonight, why don't we just play Monopoly?" She's puzzled but agrees, so the young couple sit down with the parents and play board games until midnight. When it's time to leave, the girl takes her date aside and whispers to him, "Why didn't you tell me you wanted to stay in tonight?"
"Why didn't you tell me your dad works in the chemist's?" the lad replies.

The wedding anniversary

An elderly couple are having an elegant dinner to celebrate their 75th wedding anniversary. The old man leans forward and says softly to his wife, "Dear, there's something I must ask you. It's always bothered me that our tenth child never quite looked like the rest of our children. Now, I want to assure you that these 75 years have been the most wonderful experience I could have ever hoped for, and your answer cannot take all that away. But I must know – did he have a different father?"
The wife drops her head, unable to look her husband in the eye. She pauses for a moment and then confesses, "Yes. Yes he did."
The old man is shaken – the reality of what his wife is admitting hits him harder than he had expected. With a tear in his eye he asks, "Who? Who was the father?"
Again the old woman drops her head, saying nothing at first as she tries to muster the courage to tell her husband the truth. Then, finally, she says, "You."

A: "LARGE BURGER AND FRIES, PLEASE."

Dyslexics on the piste

Two dyslexics decide to go skiing. They're just about to start up the mountain when the first one asks, "How do we get down? Do we zag-zig or zig-zag?"

"How the hell do I know?" replies the other.

So they walk up the mountain. When they reach the top they still haven't decided how to get down, so they ask a bloke: "How do we get down the mountain? Do we zig-zag or zag-zig?"

"I don't know," the man replies. "I'm a tobogganist."

"Oh, right," says the first dyslexic. "Can I have 20 B&H then?"

Doctor baffled

A man goes to see his doctor. "What seems to be the problem?" the medic asks.

"It's my penis," says the man. "I'd like you to take a look at it."

"Hop up onto the bed and whip it out," says the doc, "and I'll examine it."

So the man jumps onto the bed and produces a 12-incher from his underpants. After about five minutes peering and prodding it, the bemused doctor says, "I have to say, I can't see anything wrong with it."

To which the man replies, "I know – isn't it a beauty!"

The Buddhist's toothache

Did you hear about the Buddhist who refused the offer of Novocain during his root canal work?

He wanted to transcend dental medication.

The mark of the master

Standing at a urinal, one man turns to another.

"Excuse me," he says, "but I couldn't help noticing that you've been circumcised."

"Er, yes," says the second man, baffled. "I'm Jewish, so I was circumcised at birth."

"I guessed," says the first. "And your surgeon was Dr Abraham Winklehock – no doubt about it."

"You're right!" cries the second man, amazed. "How did you know? It was 30 years ago!"

"Bastard never could cut straight," says the first man. "And you're pissing on my shoe."

Heard it before

An Englishman, Irishman and a Scotsman walk into a bar. "What the hell is this?" the barman shouts. "Some kind of a joke?"

Anatomy lessons

What have the clitoris and the Antarctic got in common?

Most men know it's down there somewhere, but really don't care.

The big brew

An Irishman goes for a job on a building site as an odd-job man. The foreman asks him what he can do.

"I can do anything," says the Irishman.

"Can you make tea?" asks the foreman.

"Jesus, yes," replies the Irishman. "I can make a great cup of tea."

"Can you drive a forklift?" asks the foreman.

> # What do you call...
> ## ...an aardvark that's just been beaten up?
> # *A vark.*

Q: WHY CAN'T YOU HAVE DRIVING LESSONS AND RECEIVE SEX

Should have read the small print

After years of milking cows with the traditional stool-and-squirt method, Farmer Giles eventually orders a high-tech milking machine. The equipment arrives a few days later and, realising his wife is out for the day, he decides to test the machine on himself first.

After setting it up, the farmer quickly eases his beef bayonet into the equipment and flicks the switch. The sucking teat pleasures him better than his wife ever could but, when it's over, the machine will not release his member. In desperation, the farmer calls the Customer Service Hotline. "Hello," he winces, "I've just bought a milking machine from your company. It works great but, er, how do I remove it from the cow's udder?"

"Don't worry," replies the rep. "The machine will release automatically once it's collected two gallons."

"Mother of God!" replies the Irishman. "How big is the teapot?"

Doc's new career

A gynaecologist decided on a career change and signed up for a motor mechanic's course, where greasy-fingered tutors taught him how to take an engine apart and put it back together again. Following his final practical exam, the former doc anxiously awaited his results – and was pleasantly surprised when he was awarded a mark of 200%. Upon asking his examiner how this was possible, he was told that his stripping and reassemble had been perfect, earning him 100%. The additional 100% had been awarded for doing it all through the exhaust pipe.

Hard reading

Did you hear – Stevie Wonder got a cheese grater for his birthday. He said it was the most violent book he'd ever read.

The legless parrot

A man is not getting along very well with his wife, so he goes to a pet shop, hoping that having an animal to care for will bring the couple closer together. After mooching around the store he spots a parrot on a little perch. It doesn't have any feet or legs.

"I wonder what happened to you, little fella?" the man says to himself.

To his surprise, the parrot answers. "I was born this way!" the bird squawks. "I'm a defective parrot."

Paid in kind

An old lady walks into a hardware store and asks the male assistant if she can purchase a painting hung up on the wall.

The man replies, "Would you like a screw for that?" She thinks for a moment. "No," she says, "but I'll give you a blow job for a cooker."

The man is flabbergasted. "Are you telling me you understood what I said?" he asks.

"Every word," replies the parrot. "I am a highly intelligent, thoroughly educated bird."

"Oh yeah?" says the man. "Then answer me this: how do you hang onto your perch without any feet?"

"Well," the parrot says, "this is a little embarrassing, but since you asked… I wrap my twisty parrot penis around this wooden bar, like a little hook. You can't see it because of my feathers."

"Wow," the man says. "You really can understand and answer, can't you?"

"Of course. I speak both Spanish and English. I can converse with reasonable competence on almost any subject: politics, religion, sports, physics, philosophy – and I'm especially hot on ornithology. You ought to buy me. I'm a great companion!"

The man looks at the price tag. "£200!" he says. "I can't afford that!"

"Listen," the parrot hisses,

What's in a name?

A burglar is quietly going about his illegal work one night, when he hears a voice: "Jesus is watching you."
He looks around but there's no-one there, so he carries on piling swag into his bag. Then the voice speaks again: "Jesus is watching you."
Again he looks around, and this time he sees a parrot in a cage. He walks up to the cage and says: "A talking parrot, that's fantastic – are you Jesus?"
"No," replies the bird, "I'm Moses."
The thief laughs. "What kind of people would name a parrot Moses?!"
"The same people who'd call a Rottweiler Jesus," replies the bird.

motioning the guy closer with a wing. "Nobody wants me 'cause I don't have any feet. You can get me for £20, just make an offer."
So the man offers the shopkeeper £20 and walks out with the parrot. Weeks go by. The bird is sensational. He's funny, he's interesting, he's a great pal, he understands everything, sympathises, gives good advice. The man is delighted – until one day, when he comes home from work and is beckoned over by his multicoloured friend.
"I don't know if I should tell you this or not," whispers the parrot, "but it's about your wife and the postman…"
"What?" says the man.
"Well," the parrot says, "when postie came to the door today, your wife greeted him in a negligée and kissed him on the mouth."

"What happened then?" asks the man.
"Then the postman came into the house and lifted up the negligée and began fondling her naked body," reports the parrot.
"Oh no!" the man says. "Then what?"
"Then he got down on his knees and began kissing her, starting with her breasts and slowly going down and down…"
The parrot pauses. "Then what happened? What happened?" says the man, frantically.
"I don't know," says the parrot. "That's when I fell off my perch."

What's the difference…
…between a jumbo jet and a Brummie?
A jumbo jet stops whining when it gets to Majorca.

A: A LEISURE CENTRE.

Ask a stupid question...

Steve was in a terrible accident at work: he fell through a hole in the floor and ripped off both his ears. Since he was permanently disfigured, he settled with the company for a rather large sum of money and went on his way. Steve decided to invest his money in a small, but growing, telecom business. After weeks of negotiations, he bought the company outright. It was only after signing on the dotted line, however, that it dawned on him that he knew nothing about running such a business – so he set out to hire someone who could do that for him.

The next day he set up three interviews. The first guy was great. He knew everything he needed to and was very interesting. At the end of the interview, Steve asked him, "Do you notice anything different about me?"

"Why yes," the candidate answered. "I couldn't help but notice you have no ears." Steve got very angry and threw him out.

The second interview was with a woman, and she was even better than the first guy. He asked her the same question: "Do you notice anything different about me?"

"Well…" she replied, "you have no ears." Steve tossed her out.

The third and last interview, with a young man fresh from university, was the best of all three. He was smart. He was confident. And he seemed to be a better businessman than the first two put together. Steve was anxious, but went ahead and asked the young man the same question: "Do you notice anything different about me?"

To his surprise, the young man said what he wanted to hear. "Why yes – you wear contact lenses."

Steve was shocked. "What an incredibly observant young man," he said. "How in the world did you know that?"

"Well, it's hard to wear glasses with no fucking ears," replied the young man.

What's the difference...
...between a dead dog in the road and a dead lawyer in the road? *There are skid marks in front of the dog.*

The randy cheapskate

A man is wandering through a red light district when he spies a brothel advertising the best whores in town. Walking up to the front desk, he asks for the cheapest girl available and is led into a darkened room. There, he finds a woman lying on the bed – but as soon as he climbs on top and starts pumping, she repeatedly spits in his eye.

Furious, he sprints down to the front desk. "That bitch spat in my eye!" he screams at the receptionist.

The woman behind the desk calmly turns around to a bunch of men playing cards. "Get to it boys. The corpse is full."

Q: WHAT'S THE DEFINITION OF TRUST?

The rooster race

A farmer decides it is time to get a new rooster for his hens. The current rooster is still doing an okay job, but he is getting on in years, so the farmer buys a young cock from the local poultry emporium and turns him loose in the barnyard.

The old rooster sees the young one strutting around and he gets a little worried. So he walks up to the new bird and says, "You're the new stud in town? I bet you think you're hot stuff. Well I'm not ready for the chopping block yet. I'm still the better bird. And to prove it, I challenge you to a race around the hen house. Ten laps, and whoever finishes first gets to have all the hens for himself."

The young rooster is a proud bird, and definitely a match for the old guy. "You're on," says the young rooster. "And since I know I'm so great, I'll even give you a head start of half a lap."

So the two roosters start racing, with all the hens watching and cheering the two birds on. After the first lap, the old rooster is still maintaining his lead. After the second lap, the old guy's lead has slipped a little but he's still hanging in there. By the fifth lap he's barely in front of his young challenger.

By now the farmer has heard all the commotion. Thinking a fox must have broken in, he grabs his shotgun and runs into the barnyard. When he gets there, the two roosters are rounding the hen house, with the old rooster still slightly in the lead. He immediately takes aim, fires and blows the young rooster away.

"Damn!" he curses to himself. "That's the third gay rooster I've bought this month."

What's the difference...
...between a blonde and a bowling ball?
You can only get three fingers in a bowling ball.

The samurai tournament

In need of a new chief samurai, the Emperor calls together all the great dojo masters. After a huge and glorious tournament, just three champions are left: a Chinese samurai, a Japanese samurai and a Jewish samurai. In one final test, the Emperor asks the trio to prove their swordsmanship. Immediately, the Chinese samurai steps forward, unsheathes his mighty sword and it scythes through the air with a "whoosh". The onlookers gasp as a single fly falls to the floor, sliced in two.

The Japanese samurai is not impressed. Wielding his own shiny blade, he also clefts the air, and with a quick "swish" another fly falls – this time in four, precise pieces. The crowd goes wild.

Finally, it's the turn of the Jewish samurai. Smiling, he pulls out his weapon as another fly buzzes past, and there's a flurry of thrusts. The fly, however, glides happily away and out of a nearby window.

"Shame on you," grumbles the Emperor. "You failed to kill the fly."

"True," says the Jewish samurai, "but circumcision is not meant to kill."

Simple economics

A man comes home from work to find his wife in the bedroom, packing her suitcase. "What the hell are you doing?" he asks. "I'm leaving you for a better life," she replies. "I'm going to Las Vegas – I hear they pay $400 for a blow job out there." The man thinks for a minute, then gets his suitcase out and starts packing. "I'm going to Las Vegas, too," he tells her. "I want to see how you live on $800 a year."

He knows all

A Christian was wandering around town, thinking about how good his wife had been to him and how fortunate he was to have her. "God – why did you make her so kind-hearted?" he asked the Creator.

"So you could love her, my son," the Lord responded.

"Why did you make her so good-looking?"

"So you could love her, my son."

"Why did you make her such a good cook?"

"So you could love her, my son."

The man thought about all this, then he said: "I don't

What do you call...
...a woman with one leg shorter than the other?
Eileen.

mean to seem ungrateful or anything, but… why did you make her so stupid?"
"So she could love you, my son."

Lap of luxury

What has eight legs and eats pussy?
Me, you and Tatu.

Kid logic

Little Billy walked into his parents' bedroom one day, only to catch his dad sitting on the side of his bed sliding a condom onto his penis in preparation for making love to his wife.
Billy's father, in an attempt to hide his raging, condom-tipped hard-on, bent over as if he were looking under the bed. "What are you doing, dad?" asked little Billy.
"I thought I saw a rat go under the bed…" his father quickly replied.
"So what are you going to do?" said Billy. "Fuck it to death?"

The deaf newlyweds

Two deaf people get married. However, during the honeymoon, they find they're unable to communicate in the bedroom when they turn off the lights because they can't see each other using sign language. After several nights of fumbling and misunderstandings, the wife decides on a solution.
"Honey," she signs, "why don't we agree on some simple signals? For instance, at night, if you want to have sex with me, reach over and squeeze my left breast once. If you don't want to have sex, reach over and squeeze my right breast once."
The husband thinks this is a great idea and signs back to his wife, "Very clever. Now, if you want to have sex with me, reach over and pull

on my penis once. If you don't want to have sex, reach over and pull on my penis… 50 times."

Bad dog!

A man is stopped by an angry neighbour. "I'd just left the house this morning to collect my newspaper when that evil Doberman of yours went for me!"
"I'm astounded," said the dog's owner. "I've been feeding that fleabag for seven years and it's never got the bloody paper for me."

Wrong priorities

A hunter was stalking through the woods when he came across a naked lady with her legs wide open. "Are you game?" he asked her.
"Yes," she replied.
So he shot her.

What's the difference…

…between a woman in a church and a woman in the bath? *One's got hope in her soul…*

Soaks debate hobby

Two alcoholics are sat in a bar. One says to the other, "If you had the choice, which disease would you rather be struck down by – Alzheimer's or Parkinson's?" "That's a good one," slurs his chum. "It would have to be Parkinson's. I'd rather lose half my pint than forget where I put it in the first place."

WITH A CROWBAR.

What's the difference...
...between an Airfix model without adhesive and David Beckham?
One's a glueless kit...

Love Down Under

An Australian is walking down a country road in New Zealand, when he happens to glance over the fence and see a farmer going at it with a sheep. The Aussie is quite taken aback by this, so he vaults the fence and walks over to the farmer. Tapping him on the shoulder, he says, "You know, mate, back home we shear those."
The New Zealander looks round frantically. "Get lost, mate!" he says. "I'm not shearing this with no-one!"

The odd couple

Attracting more than a few raised eyebrows, a 70-year-old groom and his beautiful 25-year-old bride check into a resort hotel. Next morning at 8am sharp, the groom wanders down to breakfast whistling a happy tune. He sits at a table and, with a beaming smile to the waitress, orders bacon and eggs.
Fifteen minutes later the young bride gingerly trudges into the dining room with bowed legs – her face drawn and her hair tangled. Such is her appearance that a waitress rushes to her aid. "My God, honey, what happened?" she cries. "Here you are – a young bride with an elderly husband. But you look like you've had a fight with wild dogs."
"That bastard double-crossed me," sighs the bride. "He told me he'd saved up for 50 years. I thought he was talking about money."

The bodybuilder's tale

A man was sitting at a bar when he noticed another patron a few stools away. The guy had a body like Charles Atlas but his head was the size of a thimble. "Excuse me for staring," said the first man, "but I can't help but be curious as to why your body is so well developed but your head is so small." The bodybuilder said, "Buy me a drink and I'll tell you." So drinks were ordered and the story began. "I was in the navy and my ship was sunk by a torpedo. I was the only survivor and managed to make it to a desert island. I was sitting on the beach one day, trying to catch a fish so I would have something to eat, when I saw a beautiful mermaid sunning herself on a nearby rock. She swam over and informed me that she was a magical mermaid and could grant me three wishes. 'Great,' I said. 'I'd like to be rescued.' So she slapped

What's the difference...
...between a snow-woman and a snowman?
Snowballs.

The businessman's gamble

A blonde and a businessman are seated next to each other on a flight. "Let's play a game," proposes the man. "I ask you a question. If you don't know the answer, you pay me £5, and vice versa." The blonde isn't interested, instead preferring just to nap. "Okay, okay," insists the businessman, "you don't know the answer, you pay me £5, I don't know, I pay you £500!" Sensing no end, the blonde agrees. The businessman asks the first question: "What is the distance from the Earth to the moon?" Without even thinking, the blonde reaches into her purse, pulls out a fiver and hands it over. "Cool," says the businessman, "your turn!"

"What goes up a hill with three legs and comes down with four?" Puzzled, the businessman takes out his laptop and searches the internet for an answer. No luck. Frustrated, he sends e-mails to all his friends and co-workers, to no avail. After an hour, he wakes the blonde and hands her £500. The blonde thanks him, turns over and shuts her eyes. "Well," says the businessman, miffed, "you could at least tell me the answer." Without a word, the blonde reaches into her purse, hands over £5 to the businessman and happily drifts back to sleep.

the water with her tail and a ship appeared, sailing straight for my island. "Next I asked for a body like Charles Atlas. Another slap of the tail and here it is. "Then, noticing how beautiful she was and with all my other wishes fulfilled, I asked if I could make love to her. She said no – it just wouldn't work, her being half-fish and all. So I asked her for a little head."

The Good Samaritan

A man comes into work on a Monday with a black eye. His fellow workers ask him what happened. "I was in church yesterday," says the man, "when a young woman came in wearing a summer dress and sat in the seat in front of me. When she stood up the dress was caught between the cheeks of her bum, so I leaned forward and plucked it out. And she hit me!"

The next Monday he comes in with two black eyes. "I was in church yesterday," he explains, "and the same young woman in the same dress sat in front of me. When she stood up her dress was caught between the cheeks of her bum again, and the man beside me leaned forward and plucked it out. I knew she didn't like that, though, so I pushed it in again…"

Did you hear about… …the two lesbian twins? *They even lick alike.*

into her hairy bit." There is a muffled scream. "Dad! My head's stuck!"

The coach party

A coachload of Scousers goes screaming into a sharp bend on an icy night and everyone dies. At the Pearly Gates, Saint Peter opens up – and is horrified to see 40 of Liverpool's finest wanting to come in.

"I can't just let you all in –

Have you heard? Robert De Niro is making a film about the Harold Shipman murders. It's called The Old Dear Hunter.

Too literal

A teenage boy and his dad are alone in the house when there's a knock at the door. The boy answers it. "Dad," he says, "there's a girl at the door. She wants to come in. Shall I let her?"

"Yes, son."

"Dad, this girl wants to go upstairs. Shall I let her?"

"Yes, son."

"Dad, this girl wants to get into bed with me. Shall I let her?"

"Yes, son."

"Dad, what should I do?"

"Well – stick your hairy bit

I've got to tell the boss," he explains, and goes to check with God if it's okay. Imagining halos being used as frisbees, angels with missing wings and worse, the Lord tells Peter: "Send 'em all back but, if you must, let the first five in."

Ten minutes later, Saint Peter returns in a panic. "God," he shouts, "they've gone!"

"What, all 40?" asks the Almighty.

"No," says Peter, "the gates!"

Q: WHY DO TRAMPS STAND SO CLOSE TO RAILWAY PLATFORMS?

Man cops eyeful

A man approaches a stunning, voluptuous young woman while out shopping in the supermarket. "I'm terribly sorry," he says, "I've lost my wife – I don't suppose you'd mind talking to me for a couple of minutes, would you?"

The woman is bewildered. "Why?" she asks.

"Well," replies the man, "every time I talk to a woman with tits like yours, the old bat just seems to appear out of nowhere."

Prudent farmer

A young man was driving past a farm when he spied a pig with a wooden leg. Puzzled, he pulled in and approached the farmer: "What's the story with the pig, there?" he asked.

"That pig can recognise 100 different commands, work out mathematical equations in the dirt and speak 25 words," said the farmer.

"So what's with the wooden leg?" asked the man.

"Well," replied the farmer, "when a pig's that special, you just don't eat him all at once."

Royal fertility

Which king has had the most children?

Jonathan.

Cruel cream

A little blind girl goes up to her mum. "Mummy," she says, sadly, "when will I be able to see?"

Smiling kindly, her mum replies, "I'll tell you what, I'll take you to the chemist and get you some special cream for your eyes. You should be able to see by tomorrow morning."

With the little girl jumping around excitedly, the two head into town. They return with the cream, and that evening the mother rubs the balm onto her little girl's eyes. "Aah, mummy!" cries the girl. "It stings!"

"Be brave," consoles her mother, and wraps her head in bandages before putting her to bed.

The next morning, the little girl stumbles into her mum's bedroom. "Quick mummy," she insists eagerly, "take off the bandage!"

So, very slowly, the mother peels off the bandages, while her daughter braces herself for the magic moment. "But mummy," says the girl once the final bandage is removed, "I still can't see." Her mother grins at her sympathetically. "Yes dear," she replies. "April fool."

Literary complaint

A man visits his doctor: "Doc, I think I'm losing it," he says, "I'm forever dreaming I wrote *Lord Of The Rings*."

"Hmm. One moment," replies the doctor, consulting his medical book.

"Ah yes, now I see… you've been Tolkien in your sleep."

Blonde stumped

Deep into a game of Trivial Pursuit, it was once again the young blonde's turn to throw. She picked up the die, threw a six and landed on Science & Nature. "If you're in a vacuum and someone calls your name," asked her friend, "can you hear it?" She thought for a moment. "Right…" she replied, "is it on or off?"

A: BECAUSE WHEN A TRAIN COMES, IT'LL SUCK THEM OFF.

Desert dilemma

After a ghastly plane crash in the desert, only two men survive. They stumble across the sands for days, sunburnt and thirsty, before sighting three tents in the distance. Not knowing whether they're real or a mirage, they run towards the vision anyway. They're real! Stumbling into the first tent, they're confronted by an Arab salesman. "Water, please!" the men croak. "Do you have water?"

"Sorry, I've only got whipped cream," replies the desert-dweller.

The men tumble into the next tent and again ask for water. "Sorry, I only have custard," says the Arab sitting within.

They go into the last tent and ask for water, but again are told, "I've only got jelly. Sorry."

As the men resume their desert trek, one goes to the other, "That was weird – all that food and no water."

"Yes," comes the reply. "It was a trifle bazaar."

What's got three pairs of balls... ...and screws you twice a week? *The National Lottery.*

One-upmanship

A pro-am golf competition is taking place in Wicklow, and two amateurs are having a conversation on the first tee. The first, in a very posh voice, says, "I've reserved a rather lovely suite in the Grand Hotel. Where are you staying for the duration, old boy?"

"Jaysus," says the second amateur, "Oi'm sleepin' in the back of me Morris Minor in the Golf Club car-park."

"Really?" says the toff. "That must be rather uncomfortable."

"No, not a bit of it. Oi've a lovely king-sized double bed in the back."

WHY DO BLONDES TAKE THE PILL?

"Good Lord! Really? I have a colour TV and a bar in the back of my Rolls, but no bed."

"Well, ye'd want to get one! They're the business!" says the other fellow.

A year later, back at the pro-am competition in Wicklow, the toff glides up in his Rolls-Royce and enters the clubhouse looking for the chap in the Morris Minor. The steward directs him to the far corner of the car park. There he finds the old grey Morris, windows steamed up, rocking back and forth frenetically on its springs. Politely, the toff taps on the window. A moment later the window is wound down and the other fellow appears, looking sweaty and dishevelled.

"Hello, old boy!" says the toff. "I just popped by to tell you I've had a bed fitted in the back of the Roller."

The other fellow looks at him in disbelief and says, "You got me out of the Jacuzzi to tell me that?"

Emergency call

A man phones up the vet in the middle of the night to tell him his pet dog has swallowed a condom.

"You've got to help," he cries. "I don't know what to do."

"It is rather late," says the vet. "But as it's an emergency, I'll be there as soon as I can."

"What should I do in the meantime," says the owner.

"Just keep the dog as still as you can," says the vet. "I won't be long."

After an hour, the vet is still driving when his mobile rings. "I phoned earlier," says the caller. "My dog swallowed a condom."

"Yes, I know," says the vet. "I'm going as fast as I can, but I'm stuck in traffic."

"You needn't bother," says the dog owner. "It's okay now. We've found another one in the drawer."

Bloody kids

A kid is watching his grandfather take a piss. "Hey, Grandpa," he says. "My dad has got two of those things."

"What do you mean, son?" says the old man.

"Well, he's got a wobbly one like that for pissing through, and a long, hard one for cleaning mummy's teeth."

Salesman gets cocky

A little old lady answers a knock at her door, where a well-dressed young man carrying a vacuum cleaner greets her. "Good morning," he says, "if I could have two minutes of your time, I shall demonstrate the latest in high-powered suction."

"Bugger off," replies the old lady, moving to slam the door shut, "I haven't got any money!"

Quick as a flash, the salesman wedges his foot in and pushes the door wide open. "Now don't be too hasty, madam," he pleads, "at least see my demonstration!" And with that, he empties a bucket of manure all over her carpet. "If this vacuum cleaner doesn't remove all traces of this muck from your carpet, I'll eat the remainder."

"Then I hope you've got a bloody good appetite," says the woman, "the electricity was cut off this morning."

SO THEY KNOW WHAT DAY OF THE WEEK IT IS.

Bad day

An Englishman, an Irishman and a Scotsman were in a pub, talking about their sons. "My son was born on St George's Day," commented the Englishman. "So we called him George." "That's a real coincidence," remarked the Scot. "My son was born on St Andrew's Day, so we called him Andrew." "My God, that's amazing," said the Irishman. "The same thing happened with my son Pancake."

Mixed blessings

A police officer on a motorcycle pulls alongside a man driving around the M25 in an open-topped sports car and flags him down. The policeman solemnly approaches the car. "Sir, I'm sorry to tell you your wife fell out a mile back," he says.

"Oh, thank God," the man replies. "I thought I was going deaf."

Always finish the story

A man is very suspicious of his wife's activities, so he asks his seven-year-old son to look out for any strange men calling at the house during the day. First thing when he gets back from work, he asks his son to tell him all about what mummy has been up to. "Well," says the son, "Mr Jones from next door came round and mummy started to kiss him."

"And what happened next?" asks daddy, warming to the conversation.

"Then mummy took off all of her clothes."

"Okay, that's far enough," he says. "You can finish off the story on Saturday, when all the family are coming around."

So Saturday arrives and in the middle of the main course the man turns to his son and tells him to tell his story to everyone. "Well," says the son, "Mr Jones came round the other day and started to kiss mummy, then mummy took off her clothes and her and Mr Jones went into the bedroom."

"Yes," says the father, "now tell everyone what happened then."

"So," says the son, "Mr Jones and mummy got on the bed and started playing that funny old game you play with Aunt Maureen."

Bid for revenge

A woman wakes up and tells her husband about a dream she had. "I was at an auction for cocks – big ones sold for £1,000 and the small ones

A farmer takes his driving test... "Can you make a u-turn?" asks the instructor. "You betcha," the farmer replies. "I can make its fucking eyes water."

Q: WHAT DID ADAM SAY TO EVE WHEN HE GOT HIS FIRST ERECTION?

The busman and the banana

Ted's a bus conductor, until one fateful morning when he tells the driver to pull away as a frail old lady is boarding. Tragically, she's killed. Ted is convicted of manslaughter and, residing in Texas, faces death by the electric chair. "Any last requests?" asks the executioner.

"Well," says Ted, "I see you've an unripe banana there. Mind if I have it?" The executioner agrees, Ted polishes off the fruit and the switch is flipped – but when the smoke clears Ted is still very much alive. The authorities set him free and before long he's back on the buses… then disaster. The same accident befalls another commuter. Ted is once more sent to the chair, once more gobbles down an unripe banana and once more survives. He returns to society, and disaster strikes again: three children are pulled under the bus and it's back to the chair. Come last request time the executioner produces an unripe banana and, a few minutes later, Ted's ready. The switch is thrown, all the prison lights go out… and there's Ted, fit as a fiddle.

"Why won't you die!" screams the executioner. "It's that banana, isn't it?"

"Not at all," whimpers Ted. "I'm just a really bad conductor."

went for a tenner."

"What about one my size?" asks her man.

"Didn't get a bid," she laughs, before getting up and ready for work.

Eager to exact revenge, her husband wakes the next morning and tells his wife about a similar dream: "I was at an auction for vaginas – tight ones sold for £1,000 and flabby old loose ones for a fiver…"

"What about mine?" asks his wife, snuggling up.

"Funny you should mention it," smiles the husband. "That's where they held the auction."

A: "STAND BACK! I DON'T KNOW HOW BIG THIS THING IS GOING TO GET!"

FHM 33

What's Meg short for? Because she's got really little legs.

Bride-to-be sets out stall

After a brief, sex-free relationship, an elderly couple finally decide to marry. Before the wedding, they have a long conversation about how things might change in married life, discussing finances and living arrangements, before eventually the old man enquires about doing the wild thing.

"How do you feel about sex?" he asks, rather hopefully.

"Well," thinks his partner, "I'd have to say I like it infrequently."

The old man pauses. "I see," he says, "just to clarify, was that one word or two?"

Bursting!

Linford Christie is walking around town when he finds himself dying for a piss. Wandering over to the nearest public loo, he finds it's closed for repairs. He jogs over to McDonald's – but their dunnies are for paying customers only. Becoming ever more anxious, he trots over to a petrol station, but their shitters are being cleaned.

By now, the situation is getting critical for the Olympic medal winner, so Linford starts sprinting up the High Street looking for relief. Finally, he spies a hidden public bog, and dashes inside. Letting out a huge sigh of relief as he drains his bladder, he grins to the man in the next urinal. "Phew! Just made it!"

"Christ!" says his neighbour, glancing down, "can you make me one too?"

Underfoot crime

The authorities were called to a local housing estate last night after a man was shot in a row over a carpet. Police suspect it was rug related.

Man accompanies victim

A man is walking down the High Street when suddenly a nearby wall collapses, burying him in rubble. It's ten minutes before another passer-by – a smartly dressed man – happens to wander past.

"Christ! Are you okay mate?" he cries. "Has anyone called an ambulance?"

"Uh… no," comes the agonised reply.

"Right. Has anyone called the police?" asks the second man.

"No," moans the injured man.

"Okay… has the compensation board been informed?"

By now the injured man is groggily angry, "Look – you're the first one here!"

The smart man thinks for a minute. "All right," he says, shifting some rubble. "Move over, then."

Q: WHAT'S THE DIFFERENCE BETWEEN A PIG AND A FOX?

Englishman hails fire chief

While on a visit to New York, an Englishman decides to take a trip to Ground Zero. Spotting the local Fire Chief, he takes the opportunity to pass on his admiration and support for their excellent work. "Thank you very much," replies the fireman. "So where do you hail from?"

"Wolverhampton," replies the Englishman.

"And what state is that in?" enquires the Fire Chief.

"Oh – pretty much the same as this."

> # What's six inches long...
> ## ...and gets women excited? A £50 note.

The Irish pilots

Paddy and Mick rent a private plane for the day, and are doing fine until it's time to land. Paddy concentrates on the instrument readings and finally gets the plane down, but he has to screech to a stop to avoid running onto the grass.

"Boy, that's a short runway," Mick says, wiping the sweat from his forehead.

"Yeah," says Paddy. "But look how wide it is."

The johnny stand

A boy and his dad are at the chemist's. As they walk past the condom display the boy asks, "Dad – what are those for?"

"Son," the man replies, "they're for safe sex."

The little boy then asks why one box has only three condoms. The dad answers, "Because that is for sixth-form boys. One for Friday night, one for Saturday night and one for Sunday night." The boy then inquires why another box has six condoms. The dad explains that it is for college boys: two for Friday night, two for Saturday night and two for Sunday night.

Then the boy sees a 12-pack. "Son, that's for married men," the father explains. "One for January, one for February…"

OAP gets ideas

A Salvation Army band is merrily knocking out hymns in the local square. Soon the captain walks round with the collection box, approaching an old dear sat on the bench. "Would you like to make a donation?" he asks.

"Oh yes, of course," smiles the old lady, popping a pound into the collection.

"And for that, madam," insists the captain, "how about you select one of our hymns for yourself?"

"Ooh, really?" says the woman, delighted. "Right, I'll have him, then – the stud with the trombone."

The dog walkers

Two men walking their dogs pass each other in a graveyard. The first man says to the second, "Morning."

"No," says the second man. "Just walking the dog."

Guess the vegetable

One day a teacher brought in a bulging paper bag. "Now class," she said, "I'm going to reach into the bag and describe a vegetable, and you tell me what I'm talking about. Okay, first: it's round, plump and red."

Of course, Johnny raised his hand high, but the teacher wisely ignored him and picked Deborah, who promptly answered: "An apple."

"No, Deborah, it's a beetroot, but I like your thinking. Now for the second. It's soft, fuzzy, and coloured red and brownish…"

Johnny was hopping up and down in his seat, trying to get the teacher to call on him, but she skipped him again and called on Billy. "Is it a peach?"

"No, Billy, I'm afraid it's a potato. But I like your thinking. Here's another: it's long, yellow and fairly hard." By now Johnny was about to explode as he waved his hand frantically. But the teacher skipped him again and called on Sally. "A banana," she said. "No," the teacher replied, "it's a squash, but I like your thinking."

Johnny was pretty pissed off by now, so he spoke up. "I've got one for you, ma'am. Let me put my hand in my pocket. Okay, I've got it: it's round, hard and it's got a head on it."

"Johnny!" she cried. "That's disgusting!"

"No," said Johnny, "it's a ten-pence piece – but I like your thinking."

What's the difference...

...between a randy Swiss admiral and an efficient hoover? One sucks and sucks and never fails...

Big girl

Arnold is in bed shagging his big, fat wife when the phone rings. He answers it and says, "Could you call back later. I'm in the tub."

The crash survivor

A plane crashes over some desolate mountainous terrain. The only survivor is a Scotsman, who manages to stumble out of the wreckage and crawl, hungry and exhausted, for several miles before finding shelter in a cave. A Red Cross search party soon arrives and begins combing the mountains, looking for survivors. After a few hours, they spot the cave entrance. "Is anyone alive in there?" shouts the group leader.

"Who's that?" squawks the reply.

"Red Cross," answers the leader.

"Thank you," comes the response, "but I've already donated."

Q: WHY DO FARTS SMELL?

The bells! The bells!

A fireman comes home from work one day and tells his wife, "You know, we have a wonderful system at the fire station. Bell One rings and we all put on our jackets. Bell Two rings and we all slide down the pole. Bell Three rings and we're ready to go on the engines."

"That's super, dear," says his old lady.

"From now on," continues the firefighter, "we're going to run this house the same way. When I say Bell One, I want you to strip naked. When I say Bell Two, I want you to jump into bed. When I say Bell Three, we're going to screw all night."

So the next night the fireman comes home from work and yells, "Bell One!" and his wife takes off all her clothes. "Bell Two!" he shouts, and she jumps into bed. "Bell Three!" he barks, and they begin to screw.

But after just a couple of minutes, his wife yells, "Bell Four!"

"What's this Bell Four?" the husband asks.

"More hose!" she replies. "You're nowhere near the fire!"

A: SO THAT DEAF PEOPLE CAN ENJOY THEM TOO.

The brush of doom

An army major pops in to a field hospital to visit three sick troopers. He goes up to the first private and asks, "What's your problem, soldier?"

"Chronic syphilis, sir."

"And what treatment are you getting?"

"Five minutes with the wire brush each day."

"What's your ambition?"

"To get back to the front, sir."

"Good man," says the major, and moves on to the next bed. "What's your problem, soldier?"

"Chronic piles, sir."

"And what treatment are you getting?"

"Five minutes with the wire brush each day."

"What's your ambition?"

"To get back to the front, sir."

"Good man," says the major, and he goes to the next bed. "What's your problem, soldier?"

"Chronic gum disease, sir."

"And what treatment are you getting?"

"Five minutes with the wire brush each day."

"What's your ambition?"

"To get the wire brush before the other two, sir."

Old fogey aids golfer

After returning from the local golf course, an old man is moaning to his wife about his game. "You see, I was driving the ball pretty well," he laments, "but my eyesight's got so bad that I couldn't see where the blasted thing went."

"You're 75, Jack!" tuts his wife. "Why don't you take your brother Geoff along?"

"But he's 85 and doesn't play golf any more," replies Jack.

"Well, he does have perfect eyesight," his wife points out. "He could watch where the ball goes."

So the next day, Jack takes his brother down to the course. With Geoff looking on, his first swing sends the ball shooting down the middle of the fairway. "Did you see it?" asks Jack.

"Yup," comes the reply, "clear as a bell."

"Well, where did it go?" asks Jack, squinting into the distance.

Geoff looks at the ground. "Uh," he coughs, "I forgot."

Meeting the parents

A lad meets a girl whom he really, really likes, and soon he's invited round to meet her parents. Sitting outside their house in the car, the girl says, "Look, there's something I better warn you about. My parents are both deaf and dumb, and they have their own special way of communicating. I just don't want you to be shocked, okay?"

So it's with some trepidation that the couple enter the kitchen. Nothing could have prepared the lad for what he sees. There is the girl's mother, skirt up around her hips, shoving a bottle into her fanny, while the father is standing with his bollocks on the table and his eyes pinned open by matchsticks.

"What on earth's going on!" stutters the lad.

"I suppose I ought to

What did the plumber say...

...when he left his wife?

"It's over, Flo."

A little too much truth

An inventor was trying to sell his new computerised crystal ball to a marketing executive. As expected, the executive was highly sceptical. "Tell you what," said the inventor, "why don't you type in a question?"

The executive tapped out: "Where is my father?" The crystal ball bleeped and blooped, then finally returned an answer: "Your father is fishing in Scotland."

"Ha!" laughed the executive, "I knew this thing was rubbish – my father's been dead 15 years!"

The inventor was puzzled. "This can't be right – try asking the question in a different way."

The executive again began typing: "Where is my mother's husband?"

A short bleep later and the crystal ball returned its answer, "Your mother's husband has been dead for 15 years. Your father just landed an eight-pound trout."

---

translate," says the girl. "My mother's saying, 'Get the beers in, you cunt,' and my father's reply is, 'Bollocks, I'm watching the match.'"

The magic Coke machine

A blonde walks up to a Coke machine in a Las Vegas casino, puts in a few coins and out pops her fizzy pop. She puts some more coins into the machine, and another can of Coke pops out. She keeps putting in coins, and cans of Coke keep coming out.

A guy comes up behind her and asks to use the machine. "Piss off," she hisses. "Can't you see I'm winning?"

What's the difference... ...between a British and an Iraqi soldier? Don't know? Welcome to the United States Air Force!

Monday morning the pharmacist arrives at work to find the same guy waiting for him on the doorstep. "So?" says the chemist. "How was your weekend?"

The man replies, "Quick, I need pain relief!"

The pharmacist, knowing what the guy had been doing all weekend, says, "Are you crazy? You can't put that on your penis. The skin is way too sensitive."

"It's not for that," says the man. "It's for my arm."

"What happened?"

"Well… I drank the whole bottle of your potion," the man admits. "Then the girls never showed up."

Love potion abused

A man walks into the chemist's and tells the pharmacist, "Listen, I've got two girls coming over this weekend and they're hot, hot, hot. Would you have something to keep me going all night? It's going to be one hell of a party."

The pharmacist smiles and disappears into the back room, returning with a dusty old bottle. "This stuff is potent," he says. "Drink only one ounce of it, and I guarantee you'll be doing the wild thing all night. Let me know how it goes!"

The weekend passes and on

Almost got away with it

After watching a car weave in and out of the lanes, a police officer pulls over the driver and asks him to blow into a breathalyser. "Sorry officer," says the driver, "I can't do that – I'm an asthmatic, and I may have an attack."

"Okay, fine," replies the rozzer, "but you'll have to come down to the station for a blood sample."

The driver shakes his head. "I can't do that either. I'm a haemophiliac, so I might bleed to death."

"Well, then, we need a urine sample."

A man's best friend

A distraught man slides up to a bar and orders a double Scotch. "That's a stiff drink there, you got a problem?" asks the barman.

"Why, yes!" the man responds, "I just caught my wife with my best friend."

"That's a damn shame. What did you tell her?" enquires the barman.

"Well," says the man, "I said, 'Pack your bags wench, and get yourself out of here!'"

The barman's curiosity gets the better of him. "What did you say to your best friend?" he asks.

"That was easy," says the man. "Down, Rover! Heel boy!"

Q: HOW LONG DOES A PUBIC HAIR STAY ON THE TOILET SEAT?

"Nope, no can do – I'm also a diabetic, I'm afraid. If I do that, I'll get really low blood sugar."

Exasperated, the officer pulls open the door. "All right then," he shouts. "I'll need you to come out here and walk the white line."

"But I can't do that, officer," replies the man.

"And why the hell not?" The man furrows his brow.

"Because I'm really pissed."

Just the one pill

A man goes to see his GP. "Doc, you've got to help me," he says. "My wife just isn't interested in sex any more. Haven't you got a pill or something I can give her?"

"Look," says the doc, "I can't prescribe..."

"We've been friends for years!" pleads the patient. "Have you ever seen me this upset? I'm desperate! I can't think, I can't concentrate, my life is going to hell! You've got to help me!"

So the doctor opens his desk drawer and removes a small bottle of pills. "Ordinarily, I wouldn't do this," he explains. "These are experimental, and the tests so far indicate they're *very* powerful. Don't give her more than one, understand? Just one."

"I don't know, doc – she's awfully cold..."

"One. No more. In her coffee. Okay?"

"Um... okay." So our hero heads off for home, where his wife has dinner waiting. When dinner is finished, she goes to the kitchen to fetch the pudding. The man, in fumbling haste, pulls the pills from his pocket and drops one into his wife's coffee. He reflects for a moment, hesitates, then drops in a second pill. Now he begins to worry – the doctor did say they were powerful. Then inspiration

strikes: he drops one pill into his own coffee.

His wife returns with a crumble and they enjoy their dessert and coffee, our hero with a poorly concealed look of anticipation. Sure enough, a few minutes after they finish, his wife shudders a little, sighs deeply and heavily, and a strange smoky look enters her eyes. In a deep, throaty, near whisper, in a tone of voice he has never heard her use before, she says, "I... need... a man." His eyes glitter and his hands tremble as he replies, "Me... too."

What do you get...
...if you cross a Rottweiler with a Labrador? *A dog that scares the shit out of you then runs off with the bog roll.*

Public transport

A man with no arms or legs is waiting at a bus stop when his mate pulls up, driving a bus. "All right, Dave!" says the driver as he opens the door. "How are you getting on?"

A: UNTIL IT GETS PISSED OFF.

How many mice... ...does it take to screw in a lightbulb? *Two, but how do they get in?*

Second time lucky

A young couple are cuddling on the bed, when the boyfriend tries his luck on his loved one. But she turns round and says, "Sorry dear, but tomorrow I'm going to the gynaecologist and I want to smell fresh and nice."
At this the boyfriend turns his back, peeved at her rejection. After a short while he rolls back and taps her on the shoulder. "You don't have a dentist's appointment as well, do you?" he whispers.

Dangerous driving

An old lady, slightly mad, is wandering round the old folks home with her Zimmer on wheels. Another loony stops her in the corridor and says, "Show me your driving licence." The old woman fiddles about in her pocket and pulls out a sweet wrapper. He checks it and lets her go on her way.
Then a second man stops her and demands to see her tax disc. She presents a drinks coaster, which the lunatic checks before letting her pass on.
She carries on until she sees a third man standing with his penis hanging out. "Oh no," she mutters to herself. "Not the bloody breathalyser again."

The passenger's revenge

A man gets ripped off by a taxi driver one night, so he decides to get his own back whenever he next gets the chance. Soon after, he sees the same taxi driver, third in the cab rank. The man goes up to the first cab in the rank, gets in and tells the driver he has no money – but if he gives him a lift home he'll get a blow job in payment. The taxi driver freaks and kicks the guy out. He then goes to the second cab and makes the same offer: a blow job for a lift home. The second taxi driver also refuses, and again he gets kicked out.
So he gets into the third cab – the guy who ripped him off – and asks to be dropped off round the corner. The driver complies and drives off. As he passes the two other cabs in the rank, the passenger smiles at the other drivers and gives them both a big thumbs-up.

Dying footie fan makes last request

Having followed Manchester City his entire life, an old man lay on his death-bed with his son at his side. "Is there anything you would like me to do for you, father?" asks the son.
"Well, son," coughs his old man, "there is one thing… go and buy me a Manchester United shirt."

What do you call... ...a camel with four humps? *A Saudi Quattro.*

Q: WHY COULDN'T MOZART FIND HIS MUSIC TEACHER?

FANNY LICKING FROG INSIDE

The power of advertising

An old lady is walking down the High Street when she stops outside a pet shop. As she curiously studies the window, she notices a poster saying, "Fanny-licking frog inside."

Excited by the prospect of this, the old lady ventures inside and asks the tall, dark-haired gentleman behind the counter for more details of this mouth-watering offer. "Bonjour, Madame," replies the shopkeeper, smiling.

"But dad," protests the bloke, "after all these years as a loyal Blue, how can you turn now?"

"Trust me, son," explains his father, "far better one of them buggers dies, than one of us."

Mistaken identity

A Jewish captain and a Chinese first officer are flying together for the first time. After half-an-hour's strained silence, the captain speaks. "I don't like the Chinese."

"You don't like the Chinese?" replies the first officer. "Why?"

"Well, it was you lot who bombed Pearl Harbor."

The Chinese officer shakes his head. "We didn't bomb Pearl Harbor – that was the Japanese!" he cries.

The captain laughs, "Chinese, Japanese, Vietnamese… they're all the same to me."

There's a painful silence, before the Chinese pilot pipes up. "I don't like Jews."

"What's wrong with Jews?" growls the captain.

"Well," says the Chinese officer, "Jews sank the *Titanic*."

"No, no," corrects the captain. "The Jews didn't sink the *Titanic*. That was an iceberg."

The Oriental looks back at him. "Iceberg, Goldberg, Rosenberg… they're all same to me."

A: HE WAS HAYDN.

Hard time

A mild-mannered accountant finds himself imprisoned for tax fraud, and on his first night is escorted to his cell. When the door opens he's confronted by a six-foot skinhead covered in tattoos, staring at him from the top bunk. Terrified, the accountant curls up in the bottom bunk. After a few minutes' silence, the skinhead whispers down, "Hey, new fish – when the lights go out tonight, you and me are going to have a little game of Mummies And Daddies."

"O-o-o-okay," stammers the tax dodger.

"Which do you want to be?" hisses the skinhead. "Mummy or daddy?"

Gasping for breath, the bean counter thinks fast. "I'll be daddy."

"Guess who's sucking mummy's cock tonight…" whispers the skinhead.

Pub grub

A bloke walks into a pub and sees a sign hanging over the bar which reads: cheese sandwich £1.50, chicken sandwich £2.50, hand job £10. Checking his wallet for the necessary payment, he walks up to the bar and beckons to one of the three exceptionally attractive wenches serving drinks to an eager-looking group of men. "Yes?" she enquires with a knowing smile, "can I help you?"

"I was wondering," whispers the man, "are you the one who gives the hand jobs?"

"Yes," she purrs, "indeed I am."

The man replies, "Wash your hands, would you? I want a cheese sandwich."

Pal reprimanded

Fred arrives home from work and hears strange noises coming from the bedroom. He runs upstairs only to burst in and find his best mate pumping away with Fred's rather ugly wife. He looks at the pair in utter disgust before turning to his friend. "Honestly, Dave," he says. "I have to, but you?"

Q. WHAT'S THE DIFFERENCE BETWEEN A LIGHT BULB AND A

A brain went into a pub...

…and said, "Can I have a pint of lager please, mate?"
"No way," said the barman. "You're already out of your head."

Divorcee annoys

A judge is questioning a woman over her pending separation. "And the grounds for your divorce, madam?"

"Ooh," she replies, "about four acres, with a small stream running by…"

"No," says the judge, "I mean what is the foundation of this case?"

"Oh right," the woman continues, "well it's mainly concrete, brick and mortar…"

"No, no," the judge reiterates, "what are your relations like?"

"I have an aunt and uncle living here in town," smiles the woman, "and my husband's parents aren't far from us either."

"Dear God," pleads the judge, "let's try this as simply as we can. Do you have a grudge?"

"Oh no," says the woman, "we have a huge driveway – we've never needed one to be honest."

"Is there any infidelity in your marriage?" asks the judge, now tiring.

"Both my son and daughter have stereo sets," explains the woman, "they're always blaring out music!"

"Madam," asks the judge, sick to the back teeth, "does your husband ever beat you up?"

"Occasionally," she replies, "about twice a week he gets up about 20 minutes before me."

"That's it!" screams the judge, "why do you want a divorce?"

"Oh, I don't want a divorce," she replies, still smiling away, "my husband does – he says he can't communicate with me."

God plays golf

A man and his local vicar were playing golf. The man had a terrible time on the green and kept missing crucial three-foot putts. The third time he missed one, he exclaimed, "Fuck, missed!"

"You should curb your language, my son," the vicar commented, "or God will strike you down."

At the next hole the man missed another sitter, and again cried, "Fuck, missed!" The vicar again warned the man about the virtues of an unclean tongue.

At the next hole the man missed yet another three-footer. "Fuck!" he wailed. "Missed!"

The vicar was livid. "May God have mercy upon your soul, my son, for surely the Lord will strike you down." As he was speaking, dark clouds built up over the green, and no sooner had the vicar fallen silent than an enormous bolt of lightning forked down… and turned the vicar to ash.

"Fuck!" came a booming voice from the heavens. "Missed!"

What do you call...

...two lesbians in a closet? *A liquor cabinet.*

PREGNANT WOMAN? A: YOU CAN UNSCREW THE LIGHT BULB.

Patient troubled

After experiencing an itchy, red rash on his forehead, a man goes to see his doctor, who immediately takes a swab of the area and sends it to the lab. "They're extremely unusual results," says the doctor. "The sample contained genital DNA – basically, you have a very rare condition where a penis is growing on your forehead." Aghast, the man breaks down. "Oh my Lord, what am I going to do?" he sobs. "I'll have to give up my job… my girlfriend will leave me… and… how can I ever look in the mirror again?"

"Oh, I wouldn't worry about that," says the doctor.

"Really?" cries the man, with new hope.

"Oh yes," replies the physician. "You won't see a thing with those bollocks over your eyes."

The dreams of death

A man goes into his young son's bedroom to check he's all right. The lad is having a nightmare, so the man wakes him. The boy says he dreamt that Aunt Susie had died. The father assures the son that Aunt Susie is fine, and sends him back to bed. The next day, however, Aunt Susie dies.

A week later, the lad has another nightmare – this time that his granddad had died. The father assures his son that granddad is fine and sends him to bed, but sure enough, the next day granddad keels over and dies.

One week later, it's nightmare time once more – and this time the boy says he dreamt his daddy had died. The father assures the son that he's okay and sends the boy to bed.

The next day, the father awakes, petrified. He's sure he's going to die.

After dressing, he drives cautiously to work, fearful of a collision. He doesn't eat lunch because he's scared of food poisoning. He avoids everyone, for sure that he'll somehow be killed, jumping at every noise, starting at every movement and hiding under his desk.

Upon getting home at the end of the day, he has to unburden himself to his wife. "I've just had the worst day of my entire life!" he exclaims.

"You think your day was bad?" his wife replies. "The milkman dropped dead on the doorstep this morning."

Hunter mislays mate

A group of friends go deer hunting, separating into pairs for the day. As a huge thunderstorm rolls in, the group return to the ranch – only to spy Bill returning alone, staggering under a huge buck. "Where's Harry?" asks another hunter. "He fainted a couple of miles up the trail," Bill replies.

"You left him lying there alone and carried the deer back?"

Bill nods. "It was a tough decision," he says, "but I figured no-one is going to steal Harry."

The overenthusiastic doctor

A husband and wife are on a nudist beach when suddenly a wasp buzzes into the wife's business end. Naturally enough, she panics. The husband is also

Q: WHAT'S THE DIFFERENCE BETWEEN EROTIC AND KINKY?

quite shaken, but manages to put a coat on her, pull up his shorts and carries her to the car. Then he makes a mad dash to the doctor.

The doctor, after examining her, says that the wasp is too far in to remove with forceps. The husband will have to try and entice it out by putting honey on his dick and withdrawing as soon as he feels the wasp.

The honey is duly smeared, but because of his wife's screaming and his frantic dash to the doctor and general panic, he just can't rise to the occasion. So the doctor says he'll perform the deed if the husband and wife don't object. Naturally both

Best feet forward

A single man wanted help with the household chores, so he decided to get a pet to help out. At the pet store, he asked the owner for advice on a suitable animal. The owner suggested a dog, but the man said, "No – dogs can't do dishes."

The owner then suggested a cat, but the man said, "No – cats can't do the ironing." Finally the owner suggested a centipede. "This is the perfect pet for you," he explained. "It can do anything!" Okay, the man thought, I'll give it a try, so he bought it. Once home he told the centipede to wash the dishes. The centipede glanced over and saw piles and piles

What does an elephant...
...use as a tampon?
A sheep.

agree, for fear the wasp will do some damage, so the doctor quickly undresses, smears the honey on and instantly gets an erection, at which time he begins to plug the wife. Only he doesn't stop and withdraw but continues with vigour.

The husband shouts, "What the hell's happening?"

To which the doctor replies, "Change of plan. I'm going to drown the little bastard!"

Why do blondes...
...have big belly buttons?
From dating blond men.

of dirty dishes. Five minutes later, all the crockery was washed, dried and put away. Great, thought the man. Next he told the centipede to do the dusting and vacuuming. Fifteen minutes later the house was spotless. Wow, thought the man, deciding to push his luck.

"Go down to the shop and get me the evening paper," he told the centipede, and off it went. Fifteen minutes later, the centipede hadn't returned. Thirty minutes later and still no centipede. Forty-five minutes and the man got sick of waiting, so he went out to look for the centipede. As he opened the front door, there on the step was the centipede. "Hey, what are you doing there?" he said. "I sent you out for the paper 45 minutes ago!"

"Hold your horses," said the centipede. "I'm still putting on my boots."

A- EROTIC, YOU USE A FEATHER. KINKY, YOU USE THE WHOLE CHICKEN.

Why do elephants... ...have trunks? Because sheep don't have strings.

Kid too honest

A small child is out shopping with his dad one day, when in the madness of the sales, the two become separated. Knowing what to do, as told a thousand times before by his parents, the boy locates a shop assistant for help. "Don't worry, little fella…" the assistant happily reassures the boy, "now, what's daddy like?"

"Well…" the boy thinks for a moment, "necking lager, shagging mummy and saying 'bollocks' a lot."

Spew comes back

Two buckets of sick are strolling through the park, holding hands. Inexplicably, one starts weeping. "Whatever's the matter?" asks the other bucket. "Oh nothing…" replies her teary partner, "just fond memories – I was brought up around here."

The big question

What have a staff toilet's lavatory seat and a fanny got in common?

They're usually warm and comfortable, except you can't help wondering who's been there before you.

The super salesman

A man was handing down the family hardware store to his son. "Now Jim," the father said, "just watch as I deal with this customer." A man entered the shop and asked for a packet of grass seed. The father handed it to him and asked if he needed a lawn mower, too. "Why would I need one of those?" said the man.

"Simple," the father said, "these grass seeds grow really fast." The man accepted the deal and left £80 worse off. Now the son of the shopkeeper took over at the counter. Another customer walked in. "Could I possibly have a packet of Tampax, please," he requested.

"Certainly, sir," the young boy said. "And will you want a lawn mower with that?" The stunned man retorted, "Why?"

"Well, sir," the boy said, "you'll be doing bugger all else this weekend, so you might as well cut the grass."

Mugged by a midget

Standing at a urinal, a man notices that he's being watched by a midget. Although the little fellow is staring at him intently, the man doesn't feel uncomfortable until the midget drags a small stepladder over to him, climbs it, and proceeds to admire his privates at close

Patient troubled 2

A man walks into a surgery. "Doctor!" he cries. "I think I'm shrinking!"
"I'm sorry, sir, there are no appointments at the moment," says the physician. "You'll just have to be a little patient."

QI **WHY DON'T WORMS HAVE BALLS?**

ART & CR_ALA 2003

The tight-lipped colonel

A crusty old US Air Force Colonel finds himself at a gala event hosted by a local arts college. There is no shortage of young, idealistic ladies in attendance, one of whom approaches the Colonel for conversation. "Excuse me," says the student, "but you seem to be a very serious man. Is something bothering you?"

"No," the Colonel says, "I'm just serious by nature, ma'am."

The young lady looks at his awards and decorations and says, "It looks like you've seen a lot of action."

"Yeah, lot of action," replies the soldier.

"Look," cries the girl, angry at his taciturn nature. "You should lighten up a little. Relax. Enjoy yourself."

When the Colonel replies that he's already relaxed, the girl snaps. "Stop being so formal!" she shouts. "I mean, when was the last time you had sex?"

The Colonel looks at her. "Well, that would be 1955," he replies.

The girl cackles in triumph. "That's it," she laughs. "You've got a hang-up about sex. You need to chill out! No sex since 1955! Isn't that a little extreme?"

"Oh, I don't know," says the Colonel, glancing at his watch. "It's only 2130 now."

range. "Wow!" says the dwarf. "Those are the nicest balls I've ever seen!" Surprised and flattered, the man thanks the midget and starts to move away. But the little man stops him. "Listen, I know this is a rather strange request," says the pygmy, "but would you mind if I touched your balls?"

"Er, I suppose there's no harm in it," says the gent, glancing around.

Quickly, the midget reaches out, and tightly grips the man's testicles. "Okay," he shouts. "Now hand over your wallet or I'll jump..."

A: BECAUSE THEY CAN'T DANCE.

Wash day

A happily married couple decide that instead of mentioning sex in front of their children, they would refer to the dirty deed as "doing the laundry". One evening after dinner the husband says to his wife, "Let's go upstairs and do the laundry."
"Not now," the wife replies. "I've got a headache."
Later on whilst watching telly, the wife says:
"Darling – let's go do the laundry now."
"It's okay, honey," the man replies. "I only had a half load so I did it earlier by hand."

Closet economics

A married woman is having an affair, and whenever her lover comes over, she puts her nine-year-old son in the closet. One day, when her and her man are hard at it, the woman hears her husband's car in the driveway – so she shoves her lover in the closet as well.
"It's dark in here, isn't it?" says her little boy.
"Yes, it is," the man replies.
"Do you want to buy my cricket ball?" the little boy asks.
"No thanks," the man replies.
"Oh, I think you do," the little extortionist continues.
"Okay, okay," the man replies after considering the position he's in.
"How much?"
"Twenty-five pounds," the little boy replies.
"Twenty-five quid!" the man repeats incredulously, but has no choice but to comply. The following week the lover is back with the woman when she hears a car in the driveway, and again he finds himself in the closet with her little boy. "It's dark in here, isn't it?" the boy starts off.
"Yes, it is," replies the man.
"Want to buy a cricket glove?" the little boy asks.
"Okay, okay," the hiding lover responds, acknowledging his disadvantage. "How much?"
"Fifty pounds," the boy replies and the transaction is completed. The next weekend, the little boy's father says, "Hey, son. Go get your cricket gear and we'll get some practice."
"I can't," replies the little boy. "I sold them."
"How much did you get?" asks the father, expecting to hear the profit in terms of snails and sweeties.
"Seventy-five pounds," the little boy says.
"How much? That's extortionate! I'm taking you to the church right now!" the father explains as he hauls the child away. "You must confess your sin and ask for forgiveness."
At the church the little boy goes into the confessional box, draws the curtain, sits down and says, "It's dark in here, isn't it?"
"Don't you start that shit in here," the priest replies.

The blonde trackers

Two blondes were walking through the woods when they came to some tracks. The first blonde said, "These

What do you call...
...five Barbies in a row?
A barbecue.

Q: WHAT DOES AN ACCOUNTANT DO WHEN HE'S CONSTIPATED?

look like deer tracks." "No," said the other one, "they look like moose tracks." They argued for quite a while. In fact, they were still arguing when the train hit them.

The Brummie elephant

During his travels through the African jungle, Tarzan discovers an elephants' graveyard, where he spies one of the mighty beasts wandering around. Noticing it's an Indian elephant, Tarzan tries to make conversation. "So… you're not from around these parts, are you?" he says. "Actually," the pachyderm replies, "I'm from Birmingham Zoo, in England." Tarzan is amazed. "That's a hell of a long way to come to die," he says. The elephant looks at him. "Oh no," he responds, shaking his huge head. "I got here yesterday."

The baby-maker

An attractive young woman goes to the IVF clinic for a course of artificial insemination. The doctor tells her to go behind the screen, take all her clothes off and lie on the examination table. A few minutes later the doc joins the woman behind the screen and starts removing all of his clothes. At this the woman is obviously a little worried, so she asks what's going on. "I'm afraid we've run out of the bottled stuff," the doctor replies. "You're going to have to have draught."

Blockbuster riddle

What do the films *The Sixth Sense* and *Titanic* have in common? Icy dead people.

A: WORKS IT OUT WITH A PENCIL.

Beaten by Bill

Snow White, Arnold Schwarzenegger and Quasimodo are having a conversation. Snow White says, "Everybody tells me I am the most beautiful, divine woman that any man has ever laid his eyes on, but how do I know?"

Arnie says, "I sympathise. Everybody tells me I am the most muscular, hunky man that has ever lived, but how do I know?"

Quasimodo says, "Everybody tells me I'm the most disgusting, despicable, grotesque creature that has ever roamed the Earth, but how do I know?"

Snow White says, "Let's go and see the wise man!" So off they trot. Snow White goes in first, and five minutes later she comes out and says, "It's true. I am the most beautiful, divine woman that any man has ever laid his eyes on."

Arnie goes in, and five minutes later he comes out and says, "It's true. I am the most muscular, hunky man that has ever lived."

> ## What goes... ...down a washing line at 100mph? *Honda pants.*

Quasimodo goes in, and five minutes later he comes out and says, "Who's this Bill Gates character, then?"

Magic dad

For his homework, little Johnny is asked to write a story about a member of his family who is utterly amazing. The following day, Johnny returns to class and tells everybody his dad can eat light bulbs!

"Have you any proof, young man?" asks his teacher, somewhat disbelievingly.

"Oh yes, I heard him say it," replies Johnny. "He was in the bedroom last night with

Doctors get fruity

A man and woman are enjoying a few drinks at a bar. They soon realise they're both doctors, and after several more drinks the man decides to try his luck. "Listen," he says, "how about we go back to mine and do the wild thing tonight?"

The woman agrees, and they leave. Back at the house, the woman strips off, walks to the bathroom and starts scrubbing up like she's about to conduct major surgery. Ten minutes later she's done, and she returns to the room where the pair have sex.

"You're a surgeon, aren't you?" says the man just moments after finishing.

"I am," replies the woman. "How did you know?"

"It was the scrubbing up before we started," he says.

"Makes sense," says the woman. "You're an anaesthetist, aren't you?"

"Wow," says the man, "how on Earth did you know?"

"I didn't feel a thing..."

Q: WHAT'S A MAN'S IDEA OF FOREPLAY?

mum when he said, 'If you turn out the light, I'll eat that bloody thing…'"

The red-headed whore

A red-headed hooker decided she was doing pretty well for herself, so put on a special offer. On the inside of her left thigh she had a tattoo done of Osama Bin Laden, and on the inside of her right thigh one of George Bush, then told her clients that whoever could name these two men could pork her for free.

The next day she went out on the streets and was approached by an Arab gentleman. "If you can name these two blokes on the inside of my thighs, I'm free," she told the man as she opened her legs.

"Well, the one on the left is Osama, but I don't know who the other guy is," he

she told him.

The German sat there for a moment before replying, "I don't know who the guys are on the inside of your thighs, but the one in the middle with big lips and red hair is Boris Becker."

Supersonic!

Two aeronautic workers are painting a Concorde late one night. One man notices that the paint smells like vodka, and dares the other to take a swig. His co-worker does so and realises that the paint has some alcohol effect. Thirty pots later, the two men are pissed and stagger off their separate ways.

The next morning one of the men wakes up with the most incredible hangover. Easing himself out of bed, he finds himself being hurled halfway across the room. "What the hell!" he exclaims, as he sees wheels on his feet.

> # Why is working in an office... just like Christmas?
> ## *You do all the work, but the fat guy in the suit gets all the credit.*

confessed, so he had to pay. A little later on, an American gentleman came over. She took him to her room, stripped, opened her legs and said, "Name these two guys and you can have me for free."

"Well, the one on the right is Dubya, but I haven't a clue who the other guy is…" the man said, so he had to pay. A couple of days later a German propositioned the hooker. So she took him up to her love nest, stripped and spread her legs on the bed. "Name these two men and you can shag me for free,"

He skates to the bathroom and looks in the mirror. He has grown a long pointy nose, his shoulders have moved back and his arms have grown long and thin. At this point the phone rings – it's his drinking buddy from the day before. "What's going on?" he blurts down the line. "I've got wheels on my feet, wings instead of arms, and my head looks like a cockpit!"

"I know," says his mate. "And here's a word of warning: whatever you do, don't fart. I'm calling from America."

A: HALF AN HOUR OF BEGGING.

Bearly funny

A grizzly bear walks into a pub and says, "Can I have a pint of lager… and a packet of crisps please."

To which the barman replies, "Why the big paws?"

Organ confusion

A man walks into his local chiropodist and plants his cock on to the table.

"That's not a foot," says the chiropodist.

"I know," replies the man, "but it's a good 11 inches!"

Golf is like sex

A husband and wife love to go golfing together, but neither of them are playing like they want to, so they decide to take some private lessons. The husband has his lesson first. After the pro sees his swing, he says, "No, no, no – you're gripping the club way too hard!"

"Well, what should I do?" the man asks.

"Hold the club gently," the pro replies, "just like you'd hold your wife's breast." So the man heeds the advice, takes a swing and pow! He hits the ball 250 yards straight up the fairway. The man goes back to his wife with the good news, and the next day the wife goes for her first lesson. The pro watches her swing and says, "No, no, no – you're gripping the club way too hard."

"What can I do?" asks the wife.

"Hold the club gently, just like you'd hold your husband's penis."

The wife listens carefully to the pro's advice, takes a swing, and thump! The ball goes straight down the fairway… for about 15 feet.

"That was great," the pro says. "Now take the club out of your mouth and try it again."

The stutterer's complaint

After years of stuttering, Jim finally goes to the doctor to see if he can be cured. The doctor thoroughly examines him, and finally asks him to drop his pants – whereupon Jim's massive cock thuds onto the table. "Hmm," says the physician. "I see the problem – because of gravity, your penis's weight is putting a strain on the vocal chords in your neck."

"B-b-but wh-what c-c-can b-be d-d-done ab-b-bout i-it?" asks Jim.

The doctor smiles.

"Don't worry. Modern surgery can work miracles. We can replace your dick with one of normal size and the stuttering will

Hear about the blonde…

… who got an AM radio?

It took her a month to realise she could play it at night.

Why do Scotsmen…

…wear kilts?

Because sheep can hear a zipper a mile away.

Q: HOW DO YOU CASTRATE A PRIEST?

Blondes in space

An experimental shuttle mission blasts off for the moon with just three crew members on board: two monkeys and a blonde. As they reach orbit, Mission Control radios the craft. "Monkey No 1! Monkey No 1! Go to the control console and complete your launch checks." Quickly, the ape swings over and sits down to follow the instructions: he releases the pressure in the payload bay, lowers the temperature in engine four and balances the oxygen ratio in the reactors. Moments later, Mission Control calls again. "Monkey No 2! Monkey No 2! Go to the control console and complete your orbital tasks." The primate knuckles over and does what he's told – launching a key weather satellite and analysing solar radiation readings. An hour into the journey, Mission Control calls again: "Woman! Please go to the console." As she sits at the blinking screen, the speaker barks again. "Please complete your…" "I know…" she moans. "Just feed the monkeys, don't touch anything."

instantly disappear." Convinced, Jim agrees to the op – and, as the doctor promised, his stuttering completely stops afterwards. Three months later, however, he returns to the doctor's surgery. "Doc, I'm still grateful for what you did," he says, "but my wife really misses my big dick. So I've decided I'll live with stuttering for the rest of my life, and get my old dick back." The doctor shakes his head, sadly. "Hey," he says, "A d-d-d-deal's a d-d-deal."

A: KICK THE ALTAR BOY IN THE BACK OF THE HEAD.

> # Why do female paratroopers...
> ## ...wear jockstraps?
> *So they don't whistle on the way down.*

Multiple birth

A young lady in a maternity ward is asked by the midwife if she would like her husband to be present at the birth. "I'm afraid I don't have a husband," she replies. "Okay – do you have a boyfriend?" asks the midwife.

"No, no boyfriend either."

"Do you have a partner then?"

"No, I'm unattached, I'll be having my baby on my own." After the birth the midwife again speaks to the young woman. "You have a healthy bouncing baby girl, but I must warn you before you see her that the baby is black."

"Well," replies the girl. "I was very down on my luck, with no money and nowhere to live, and so I accepted a job in a porno movie. The lead man was black."

"I see," says the midwife. "I'm sorry that I have to ask you these awkward questions, but I must also tell you that the baby has blonde hair."

"Well yes," the girl replies. "You see, there was this Swedish guy also involved in the movie. I needed the money – what else could I do?"

"Oh, I'm sorry," the midwife says. "That's really none of my business. I hate to pry further, but your baby has Oriental eyes."

"Well yes," continues the girl. "I was incredibly hard up and there was a Chinese man also in the movie. I really had no choice."

At this the midwife again apologises, collects the baby and presents her to the girl, who immediately gives the baby a slap on the bum. The baby starts crying and the mother exclaims, "Thank God for that!"

"What do you mean?" asks the midwife, shocked.

"Well," says the girl, extremely relieved, "I had this horrible feeling that the little bastard was going to bark."

What's in a name?

A bloke is on an aeroplane when he sees a beautiful woman sitting across the aisle. He notices that she's reading a magazine article about penis size, so he decides he'd better introduce himself. He walks across and says, "What you reading?"

"Well," she says, "it says here that Native Americans have the thickest cocks of all men. And it also says that Polish men have the longest cocks of all men. Oh, I'm sorry, I didn't get your name..."

"Tonto Kowalski," he smiles.

Q: WHAT DOES A POSTCARD FROM A BLONDE ON HOLIDAY SAY?

Sex education

Sammy came running into the house and asked, "Mummy, can little girls have babies?"

"No," said his mum, "of course not."

So he ran back outside. "It's okay," his mum heard him say to the girl next door. "We can play that game again!"

Fly killer on ball

A lady walks into the kitchen where her husband is busy killing flies with the swatter.

"Any luck?" she asks.

"A bit," he replies, "I've killed three males and two females."

Intrigued, she asks how he could possibly know the sex.

"Easy," he responds, "three were sitting on my beer can and the other two were on the phone."

What's the similarity...
...between the KGB and oral sex?
One slip of the tongue and you're in the shit.

Mutt enjoys flick

A man visits his local cinema. Throughout the film, he notices that a young chap in front has brought his dog along – and what's more the hound is laughing and crying at all the relevant places. The film finishes and, gripped by curiosity, the man wanders over to the pair.

"I couldn't help but notice," he says to the chap, "but your dog laughed at all the funny bits and cried at all the sad bits… it's amazing! I just can't believe it!"

"I can't believe it either," replies the man, "he hated the book."

The prodigal sons

Four middle-aged men are telling stories in a bar. While one has gone for a piss, the first guy says, "I was worried that my son was going to be a loser, because his first proper job was washing cars on a garage forecourt. But it turns out he got a break, they made him a salesman, and he sold so many motors that he bought the dealership! In fact, he's so successful that he just gave his best friend a new Mercedes for his birthday."

The second man says, "I was worried about my son too, because he started out tidying gardens for a lettings agency. Turns out he got a break, they made him a salesman, and he eventually bought the firm. In fact he's so successful that he just gave his best friend a new house for his birthday."

The third guy says, "I hear what you're saying. My son started out sweeping floors in a bank. He got a break, they made him a trader, and now he owns the company. In fact, he's so rich that he just gave his best friend £1m in shares for his birthday."

The fourth bloke comes back from the toilet. The first three explain that they are telling stories about their sons, so he says, "Well, I'm embarrassed to admit that my son is a major disappointment. He started out as a hairdresser – and is *still* a hairdresser after 15 years! In fact I just found out that he's gay and has several boyfriends. But I try to look on the bright side: his boyfriends just bought him a new Mercedes, a new house and £1m in shares for his birthday."

The three ducks

A farmer walks into a pub with his three favourite ducks. He says to the barman, "I'll have a pint of Guinness please."

So the barman starts to pour the farmer's pint. Whilst it's settling the farmer says to the barman, "If I show you a trick, can I have my pint for free."

The barman looks at the farmer and says, "Well, it'll have to be something special for a free pint."

"Just go and talk to my three ducks and you'll see how special it is," says the farmer. So the barman walks over to the ducks.

"Hello, first duck, what's your name?"

"My name's Stanley," replies the first duck.

"And what have you been up

The clumsy lumberjack

Sam and John were out chopping wood when John cut his arm off. Sam wrapped the severed arm in a plastic bag, then drove it and his bleeding buddy to the nearest surgeon. "You're in luck!" the surgeon exclaimed. "I'm an expert at reattaching limbs – come back in four hours." When Sam returned the surgeon said, "I got it done faster than I expected to. John's down the pub." Overjoyed, Sam ran to the pub, where John was fit and well and playing darts. A few weeks later Sam and John were out again, and this time John chopped his leg off. Sam put the leg in a plastic bag and took it and John back to the surgeon. "Legs are a little tougher," said the medic. "Come back in six hours."

Sam returned at the allotted time and the surgeon said, "I finished early – John's down the park." Sam headed off and there was John, playing football, good as new. A few weeks later, John had a terrible accident and cut his head off. Sam put the head in a plastic bag and drove it and the rest of John to the surgeon. "Heads are really tough," said the bone-cutter. "Come back in 12 hours." When Sam returned, he was met by a glum-faced surgeon. "I'm sorry," he said, "John died." "I understand," said Sam, "heads must be tough." "No, the surgery went fine," explained the doc. "But he suffocated in that plastic bag."

Q: WHAT'S AN AUSTRALIAN'S IDEA OF A BALANCED DIET?

What's the worst thing...
...about being a test-tube baby?
You know your dad's a wanker.

to today, Stanley?"

"It's been raining all day and I've been jumping in and out of puddles. It's been great."

"And what's your name, second duck?" asks the barman.

"My name is Jeremy," replies the second duck.

"And how are you, Jeremy?"

"Fine, thank you – it's been raining all day and I've been jumping in and out of puddles."

The barman approaches the third duck, noticing that he doesn't look as happy as Stanley and Jeremy. "Hello, third duck," he says. "And what's your name?"

"Puddles," says the duck. "Don't ask."

What do you call...
...a hotel lobby full of chess experts bragging about how good they are?
Chess nuts boasting by the hotel foyer.

MD makes choice

To cut costs, a managing director is forced to sack an employee. After much thought, he narrows it down to just two people: young Debbie and young Jack. Both have near identical performance records and it's a tough decision. After hours of deliberation, he's still undecided, so he makes it simple on himself. The first person to the water cooler on Monday morning gets the sack.

Monday arrives and Debbie walks in with a monstrous hangover. After a few minutes she's at the water cooler. Slowly, the MD wanders over: "Debbie, I'm so sorry," he says, "I've never had to do this before but due to powers beyond my control, I've got to lay you or Jack off."

"I see," says Deborah, "could you jack off then? I've an awful headache this morning…"

Cheese explained

What do you call cheese that isn't yours?
Nacho cheese.

Intake healthy

How do you know you have a high sperm count?
Your girlfriend chews before swallowing.

What do prawns and women... ...have in common? Three pink bits that taste nice, but the heads are full of shit.

The sailor's parcel

Just after getting married, a sailor is informed his next naval posting will be a remote Pacific island. A few weeks after arriving, he begins to miss his new wife, and so writes her a letter. "My love," he writes, "we will be apart for a year – far too long. Already I'm missing you and there's really not much to do here. Worse, we're constantly surrounded by young, nubile native girls. Do you think if I had a hobby of some kind I would not be tempted?" A few weeks later, a parcel arrives from his wife, containing a harmonica and a note, saying, "Why don't you learn to play this?" Several months later, his tour of duty ends and he rushes back to his wife. "Darling," he cries, "I can't wait to get you into bed so that we can make passionate love!" The wife frowns at him. "First things first," she replies. "I want to see you play that harmonica."

The holy round

God and Saint Peter are playing golf, and it's level pegging as they reach the 18th hole. God steps up to the tee and belts his ball. It hooks wide into the trees... but a few seconds later a rabbit runs out onto the fairway with God's ball in its mouth, attempting to eat it. While the rabbit is chewing at the ball, a hawk flies overhead and swoops down on the bunny, picking it up with its claws and flying back up again. From a hut just inside the woods runs a hunter, who loads his weapon, aims and shoots the hawk out of the sky. The hawk's crumpled body falls out of the sky, still holding onto the rabbit, and lands right next to the 18th hole. The ball rolls out of the deceased rabbit's mouth to give God a hole in one. "Are we here to play golf," asks Saint Peter, "or are You just going to fuck around?"

On top of the tower

Three pissed-up blokes stood on top of the Eiffel tower. The first one said, "I bet you I could jump off this tower and bounce all the way back up."
The second bloke said that it was impossible and taunted the first to have a go. With that the first bloke leapt off the tower, fell to the bottom and bounced back up.
The second bloke was amazed, and said he'd try it for himself. So he leapt from the tower... and fell to his death on the cobbles below. With that the third bloke turned to the first and said, "You're a right bastard when you're pissed, Superman."

Q: DID YOU HEAR ABOUT THE DYSLEXIC DEVIL-WORSHIPPER?

Ask a silly question...

After getting a job at the income tax office, a young financial hotshot is given his first assignment: auditing a rabbi. Arriving at the synagogue, he decides to have some fun. "Rabbi," he begins. "What do you do with the drippings from the candles?"

"Well," the elderly rabbi replies, startled, "we send them to the candle factory, and every once in a while they send us a free candle."

"And what do you do with the crumbs from your table?" asks the taxman. The rabbi looks at him, surprised. "Well, we send them to the matzo ball factory, and every once in a while they send us a free box of matzo balls."

Nodding, the young hotshot turns to his final question. "So tell me," he asks, steepling his fingers, "what do you do with the foreskins from circumcisions?"

By now, the rabbi's had enough. "Well, we send them to the income tax office," he answers patiently. "And every once in a while they send us a little prick like you."

The newlyweds' rules

Two newlyweds are in their honeymoon suite, when the groom decides to let the bride know where she stands right from the start of the marriage. He proceeds to take off his trousers and throw them at her. "Put those on," he says.

The bride replies, "I can't wear your trousers."

He replies, "And don't forget it! I'll always wear the trousers in this family!"

So the bride takes her knickers off and throws them at him with the same request, "Try those on!"

"I can't get into your knickers," he says.

"And you never bloody will," she snorts, "if you don't change your attitude."

A. HE SOLD HIS SOUL TO SANTA.

A busy day in Heaven

Three men were standing in line to get into Heaven. It had been a pretty busy day, however, so Saint Peter had to tell the first one: "Heaven's getting pretty close to full and I've been asked to admit only people who have had particularly horrible deaths. What's your story?"

The first man replied: "For a while I've suspected my wife has been cheating on me, so today I came home early and tried to catch her red-handed. As I came into our 25th-floor flat, I could tell something was wrong, but all my searching around didn't reveal where this other guy could have been hiding. Finally, I went out to the balcony, and sure enough there was this man hanging

"That sounds like a pretty bad day to me," said Peter, and let the man in.

The second man came up and Peter explained to him about Heaven being nearly full, and again asked for his story. "It's been a very strange day," he began. "You see, I live on the 26th floor of a building, and every morning I do my exercises out on my balcony. Well, this morning I must have slipped or something, because I fell over the edge. But I got lucky, and caught the railing of the balcony on the floor below me. I knew I couldn't hang on for very long, when suddenly this man burst onto the balcony. I thought I was saved, but he started beating me and kicking me! I held on for as long as

> **How many blondes...**
> **...does it take to make chocolate chip cookies?**
> *Six. One to stir the mixture, five to peel the Smarties.*

off the railing, 25 floors above ground! By now I was really mad, so I started beating him and kicking him, but wouldn't you know it, he wouldn't fall off. So finally I went back into my apartment and got a hammer and starting hammering on his fingers. Of course, he couldn't stand that for long, so he let go and fell – but he landed in the bushes, stunned but okay. I couldn't stand it any more, so I ran into the kitchen, grabbed the fridge and threw it over the edge, where it landed on him, killing him instantly. But all the stress and anger got to me. I had a heart attack and died there on the balcony."

I could, until he ran into the flat, grabbed a hammer and started pounding on my hands. Finally I just let go, but again I got lucky and fell into the bushes, stunned but all right. Just when I was thinking I was going to be okay, this refrigerator comes falling out of the sky and crushes me instantly, and now I'm here."

Once again, Peter had to concede that that sounded like a pretty horrible death, and in he went.

Then the third man came to the front of the line, and again the whole process was repeated. "Picture this," said the third man. "I'm hiding naked inside a refrigerator…"

HOW IS A WOMAN LIKE A LAXATIVE?

What have Arsenal and a three-pin plug... ...got in common? *They're both useless in Europe.*

Quickie pays off handsomely

A teenage girl confesses to her mother that she's missed her period for two months running. They immediately purchase a home pregnancy test, and the result's confirmed – she's up the duff. "Bring me the pig who did this to you!" screams her incandescent mother.

"I want to see him, now!" The girl quickly makes a phone call to her lover, and half an hour later a gleaming, brand new Ferrari pulls up outside the house. Out steps a mature and distinguished gentleman, handsome and impeccably dressed. He enters the house and sits down in the living room with the father, mother and the girl.

"Good afternoon," he politely greets the family, "your daughter has informed me of the situation. I am unable to marry her due to my personal family circumstances, but rest assured, I'll take full responsibility. If a girl is born, I'll bequeath her three of my shops, two townhouses, a beach house and a £1m bank account. If it's a boy, my legacy will be two factories and a £2m bank account. If it's twins, a single factory and £500,000 each. However, if there is a miscarriage…"

The father, breaking his stunned silence, places a hand firmly on the man's shoulder: "You'll shag her again, right?"

Should have listened

A secretary answers the phone in a busy office. "Good morning, Nottingham Parachute Club," she says.

There's a sharp intake of breath. "Excuse me," says a man on the other end of the line, obviously startled. "But don't you mean the Nottingham Prostitute Club?"

"Oh no, sir," laughs the secretary, "it's definitely a parachute club."

"Damn!" says the man. "Last week your salesman called and signed me up for two jumps a week."

A man walks into a bar...

...with an ostrich and a cat. The man buys the first round, the ostrich buys the second round, but when it's the cat's round the moggie refuses to pay. The bartender asks the man what the problem is. "I met a genie and he gave me one wish," explains the man, sourly. "So I wished for a bird with long legs and a tight pussy."

A: THEY BOTH IRRITATE THE SHIT OUT OF YOU.

A wig and a turd...
...walk into a bar, where the wig orders two pints of lager. When the barman refuses to serve him, the wig asks why. *"Because you're off your head,"* replies the barman, *"and your mate's steaming."*

The potato daughters

One evening, the women in the Potato Head family were getting dinner ready – mother Potato Head and her three daughters. Midway through the preparation of the meal, the eldest daughter spoke up. "Mother?" she said. "I have an announcement to make."

"And what might that be?" said mother, seeing the obvious excitement in her eldest daughter's eyes.

"Well," replied the daughter, "I'm getting married!"

The other Potato daughters squealed with surprise as Ma Potato exclaimed, "Married! That's wonderful! And who are you marrying, eldest daughter?"

"I'm marrying a Russet!"

"A Russet!" replied mother Potato with pride. "Oh, a Russet is a fine tater, a fine tater indeed!"

As they got back into preparing dinner, the middle daughter spoke up. "Mother? I, too, have an announcement."

"And what might that be?" encouraged mother Potato. The middle daughter paused, then said with conviction, "I, too, am getting married!"

"You, too!" mother Potato said with joy. "That's wonderful! Twice the good news in one evening! And who are you marrying, middle daughter?"

"I'm marrying a King Edward!" beamed the middle daughter.

"A King Edward!" said mother Potato with joy. "Oh, a King Edward is a fine tater, a fine tater indeed!"

Once again the kitchen came alive with laughter and excited plans for the future, when the youngest Potato daughter interrupted. "Mother? Umm... I, too, have an announcement to make."

"Yes?" said mother Potato with great anticipation.

"Well," said the youngest Potato daughter with the same sheepish grin as her sisters before her, "I hope this doesn't come as a shock to you, but I am getting married as well!"

"That's wonderful. Who are you marrying?" asked mother Potato Head.

"I'm marrying John Motson!" the youngest Potato daughter replied.

"John Motson!" shrieked mother Potato. "But he's just a common tater!"

Q: WHAT DID THE LEPER SAY TO THE PROSTITUTE?

Refugees assisted

A driver spies a refugee eating grass along a stretch of motorway. He pulls over. "Hey, don't eat that," he shouts, "it's filthy! Full of dog shit, road grit, all sorts. If you're hungry, come along home with me!"

The refugee looks up and replies: "I have a wife also…"

"No problem," says the man, "bring her as well, the more the merrier!"

"I also have eight children, two grandchildren and many cousins," the refugee continues.

"Now wait a minute," shouts the man, readying his engine, "just how big do you think my bloody lawn is!"

The three hookers

Three tarts are sitting up at the bar. The first prossie says, "I bet you a fiver I can put my three fingers up my fanny."

The second hooker pipes up, "I've had so much sex, I bet I can put a whole fist up mine."

The third says nothing and simply slides down the bar-stool.

A: YOU CAN KEEP THE TIP.

What do you call...
...an anorexic with a yeast infection?
A quarterpounder with cheese.

The thirsty grasshopper

A grasshopper walks into a pub and asks for a pint. As the landlord is pulling the beer he says to the grasshopper, "We've got a cocktail named after you here."

"What?" says the grasshopper. "You've got a cocktail called Steve?"

The mystery of the tunnel

An Irishman, an Englishman and Claudia Schiffer were sitting in a train carriage when the loco plunged into a tunnel. As it was an old-style train, there were no lights in the carriages, and it went completely dark. Then there was a kissing noise, followed by the sound of a really loud slap.

When the train came out of the tunnel, Claudia Schiffer and the Irishman were sitting as if nothing had happened. The Englishman, however, had his hand against his reddening cheek. The Englishman was thinking: "The Irish fella must have kissed Claudia Schiffer, but she missed him and slapped me instead." Claudia Schiffer was thinking: "The English fella must have tried to kiss me and actually kissed the Irishman, and got slapped for it."

And the Irishman was thinking: "This is great. The next time the train goes through a tunnel, I'll make another kissing noise and slap that English bastard again."

The oldsters' breakfast

An elderly couple had been married for 50 years. They were sitting at the breakfast table one morning when the old gentleman said to his wife, "Just think, darling, we've been married for half a century."

The quick thinking explorer

Two polar explorers are walking in the Arctic when all of a sudden a ferocious polar bear comes charging towards them. "Oh shit!" says the first explorer, panicking. "What are we going to do?" The second explorer says nothing, but calmly takes off his backpack, puts on a sweat-band and shorts, takes off his snow-shoes and slips on a pair of trainers. The first explorer turns to him and gabbles, "You're mad! There's no way you'll outrun a polar bear!"

"You're right," replies the second man. "But I'll sure outrun you."

Q: WHAT TYPE OF BEES PRODUCE MILK?

The three nutters

The Queen visits a mental hospital. Walking into the first ward, she's greeted by a patient sitting up in bed. With his left hand he seems to be grabbing something from the air.

"What are you doing, young man?" asks Her Maj.

"I'm taking the stars from the sky!" replies the patient. Moving swiftly on, the Queen walks over to the second patient. He too is sitting bolt upright in bed, but this time he seems to be inserting something into the air.

"What are you doing, young man?" asks the regent, politely.

"I'm putting the stars back in the sky!" babbles the second patient.

Chastened, she reaches the third patient. He's sitting up, gripping an imaginary steering wheel and making high-speed noises.

"And what exactly are you doing?" asks the Queen, wearily.

"I'm trying to get away from those two nutters," the patient gabbles. "They're mental!"

"Yes, dear," she replied. "Just think, 50 years ago we were sitting here at this breakfast table together."

"I know," the old man said. "And we were probably sitting here naked, too."

"Well," granny snickered, "what do you say? Should we get naked again?"

Whereupon the pair stripped to the buff and sat back at the table.

"How does that feel?" asked the man.

"You know, sweetheart," the little old lady replied, breathlessly, "my nipples are as hot for you today as they were 50 years ago."

"I'm not surprised," replied gramps. "One's in your coffee and the other's in your porridge."

Twice is nice

Two old men are comparing their sex lives. "I can still do it twice!" claims the first man.

"Which time do you enjoy the most?" inquires the second.

"I think the winter," he replies.

The absent brothers

An Irishman walks into a pub and orders three pints of Guinness, taking a sip out of each pint in turn. The barman says to him, "A pint goes flat after I pull it – it'd be better if you bought one at a time." The Irishman replies, "Well, I have two brothers, one in America and the other in Australia. We promised we'd all drink this way to remember the days we supped together."

Over the weeks the Irishman becomes a regular and always buys his drinks three at a time, until one day, when he orders just two pints. The other drinkers fall silent. "I don't want to intrude on your grief," says the barman when the Irishman comes back for a second round, "but I wanted to say I'm sorry about your loss."

"Oh, no," says the Irishman, "my brothers are fit and well. It's just that I've given up drinking."

Thanks for the advice

Barely 20 minutes after teeing off, a woman stumbles into the golf course clubhouse, grimacing in pain. "What happened?" the club pro asks.

"I got stung by a bee," she replies.

"Where?"

"Between the first and second holes."

"Hmmm," murmurs the pro. "Sounds like your stance was a little too wide."

Footballer enjoys welcome

After finally negotiating a professional contract, a striker arrives for his first match at his new Premiership club. "I'll tell you what," says the coach. "As it's your first game, you can play for 45 minutes then I'll pull you off at half-time."

"That's not bad," the lad replies. "I only got half an orange at my old place."

Q: WHY DID THE WOMAN CROSS THE ROAD?

What's the similarity...
...between a rural jog and Delia Smith?
One's a pant in the country...

The dyslexic redneck

In a tiny shack in Louisiana, Mary-Jo has gone into labour – and the baby is coming fast. Her husband Billy Bob dials 911 and asks for help. "Certainly," says the emergency operator, "we'll send the paramedics straight out to you. Just tell me where you live."

Billy Bob thinks for a second. "On Eucalyptus Drive," he drawls.

"Can you spell that for me?" asks the operator.

There's a long pause. "Tell ya what," Billy Bob says, furrowing his brow, "I'll drag her onto Oak Street. Pick her up from there."

The helpful wife

A man and his wife are driving down the motorway when a copper pulls them over. "What's the problem, officer?" says the man. "You were going at at least 95mph," says the traffic cop. "Nooo," replies the motorist, "I was only doing 75."

"Oh, Harry," pipes up the wife. "You were doing 95." The man glares at his wife. "I'll also have to give you a ticket for a broken rear light," says the policeman. "Broken light?" says the man. "I didn't know anything about a broken light."

"Oh, Harry," says the wife, "you've known about that tail-light for months!" The man gives his wife another foul look.

"I'll also have to write you up for not wearing your seat belt," continues the cop. "Seat belt?" says the man. "I just took it off when you were walking up to the car…"

"Oh, Harry," says the wife. "You know you never wear your seat belt."

At this the man finally cracks. "Shut up, you stupid bitch!" he screams.

The officer turns to the woman and asks, "Does your husband always talk to you this way?"

"Oh, no," says the wife. "Only when he's drunk."

The Barbie pricelist

A man walks into Toys-R-Us and says to the sales assistant, "Could you show me your Barbie dolls, please?"

"Certainly, sir," she says. "Here, we have Fashion Barbie at £15.95, Vacation Barbie, also £15.95, Housewife Barbie – that's £15.95 too – and Divorcee Barbie, at £215.95."

The man is astonished. "Why's Divorcee Barbie so much?" he asks. "She looks the same as the others to me."

"Well, sir," says the assistant, "that's because Divorcee Barbie comes complete with Ken's car, Ken's house, Ken's furniture, Ken's dog…"

A: NEVER MIND THAT – WHAT IS SHE DOING OUT OF THE KITCHEN?

The life of Jesus

A Sunday School teacher was concerned that his young students might be a little confused about the life of Jesus Christ. He wanted to make sure they understood that the birth of Jesus occurred a long time ago, so he asked his class, "Where is Jesus today?" Little Stevie raised his hand and said, "He's in Heaven." Mary was called on and answered, "He's in my heart."

Johnny, waving his hand furiously, blurted out, "I know! I know! He's in our bathroom!"

The whole class went very quiet, looked at the teacher and waited for a response. The teacher was at a loss for a few very long seconds. Finally, he gathered his wits and asked Johnny how he knew this.

"Well, every morning my dad gets up, bangs on the bathroom door and yells, 'Jesus Christ! Are you still in there?'"

OJ's collection

A man is driving along the freeway in Los Angeles. As he reaches the downtown area he finds himself in the middle of a massive traffic jam, blocking up five different freeways and sending lines of cars back for miles in all directions. After a while, he notices a guy walking from car to car down the freeway, stopping and talking to people. When the guy reaches him he rolls down his window and says, "Hey! What's causing all this delay?"

The pedestrian says, "Well, you're not going to believe this, but OJ Simpson has sat down in the middle of the freeway intersection up there, and he's totally distraught. He says there's no way he can ever pay the $35 million he owes the Goldmans and the Browns, so he's threatened to douse himself in gasoline and set himself alight if people don't give money sufficient to cover the cost of the judgement. I've taken up a collection to try to end the traffic jam."

"How much have you got so far?" asks the motorist.

"About ten gallons."

> # Why aren't blondes...
> ## ...good cattle herders?
> *Because they can't even keep two calves together.*

Kids – bless 'em

A little boy walks into the bathroom as his dad is just about to get into the shower. He looks up and points at his father's waist and says, "Daddy, daddy, what's that?"

To which his father replies, "Oh, er… that's my hedgehog, son."

The kid thinks for a moment, then says, "Wow! He's got a big cock, hasn't he?"

Q: WHERE WOULD YOU FIND A DUCK WITH NO LEGS?

Sporting condition

While out jogging in the park, a young chap happens upon a brand new tennis ball. Seeing nobody around to claim it, he slips it into the pocket of his shorts and continues on.

A few roads from home, he reaches a pedestrian crossing. Waiting for the traffic to stop, a young lady standing next to him can't help but notice the considerable bulge in his shorts. "Oh my," she gasps, "whatever is that in your shorts?"

"Tennis ball," replies the man, still breathless from exercise.

"Oh, poor you," sympathises the woman. "I once had tennis elbow."

Fergie accosted

Sir Alex Ferguson is a guest of honour at the Miss World contest. During the interval, the judges and contestants are mingling over drinks when Sir Alex is besieged by the voluptuous Miss Venezuela. "Sir Alex, I admire your management skills and all you have achieved and the trophies you have won," the beauty says. Sir Alex is flattered, then bowled over as the Venezuelan belle lowers a shoulder strap, revealing her left breast. "Would you autograph this please?" Bemused, Sir Alex nevertheless duly obliges, makes his excuses and wanders off. Moments later, the equally beautiful Miss Croatia approaches him. "Sir Alex," she blushes, "I so admire the way you play mind games with your opponents even before you meet them on the pitch." Acknowledging the compliment, Sir Alex is about to thank the girl when she lowers a strap and presents her right breast to him: "Would you be so kind as to autograph this?"

Sir Alex again obliges, mumbles an excuse and makes for the bar – where Miss Argentina taps him on the shoulder. "Oh, Sir Alex, how I admire the way you motivate your players and shield them like they're your own sons," she gushes. But before Sir Alex can do or say anything, the South American ups her dress, pulls aside her knickers and asks, "Would you do me the honour of signing this?"

"You must be joking, hen!" laughs Sir Alex. "The last time I signed an Argentinian twat, it cost me £28 million!"

How can you tell...

...if it's your turn to do the washing up? *Look down your trousers. If you've got a dick, it's not your turn.*

The drowning presidents

Richard Nixon, Jimmy Carter and Bill Clinton are on the *Titanic*. When it starts to sink, Carter yells, "Quick! Save the women and children first!"

Nixon shouts, "Fuck the women and children!"

To which Bill replies, "Do we have time?"

WHERE YOU LEFT IT.

The magic diddle

A little boy is casually walking along the upstairs landing when he happens to see his older sister's door partially open. Glancing inside he notices his sister moaning in the throes of ecstasy whilst fingering herself, uttering the words, "I want a man!" over and over again.

The little boy hastily goes downstairs to watch television, slightly confused by the incident.

A couple of hours later he's disturbed by groaning and grunting noises from the landing. He dashes upstairs and sees through the crack in his sister's door that her boyfriend is banging her senseless.

On seeing this, the little boy dashes into the bathroom, pulls down his kecks and starts pulling away, muttering to himself, "I want a bike, I want a bike!"

Pirate in the wars

A pirate walks into a tavern. "Haven't seen you in a while," says the barman, "what happened? You look terrible!"

"What do you mean?" replies the pirate.

"Well, you never had the wooden leg before," says the barman.

"Oh… we were in a battle and I got hit on the knee by a cannonball," says the pirate.

"Well what about that hook?" asks the barman.

"Another battle," says the pirate. "Enemy captain came at me with a sword and cut it clean off. So I got this hook."

"I see," says the barman, "and the eye-patch?"

"A bird flew over and shat in my eye," replies the pirate.

"You're kidding!" roars the bartender. "You lost an eye from a bird shitting in it?"

"Not quite," says the pirate. "It was my first day with the hook."

What's the difference…

…between Israeli soldiers and Dwight Yorke? *Israeli soldiers knew when to pull out of Jordan.*

Child ponders human biology

A young boy was feeling inquisitive. "Mum, is it true that people can be taken apart like machines?"

"Of course not, sweetie," she replied, "where on Earth did you hear such nonsense?"

"From daddy," said the boy. "He was talking to someone on the phone the other day and said he was screwing the arse off his secretary."

Library causes pain

A man is horribly run over by a mobile library. The van screeches to a halt, the man still screaming in agony with his limbs torn apart. The driver's door opens, a woman steps out, runs over to the victim, leans down and whispers, "Ssshhhhh…"

Q: WHAT DO ESSEX GIRLS USE FOR PROTECTION DURING SEX?

Fear the pretzel!

It's the final of the wrestling at the Olympics, and the field has been narrowed down to a Russian and an American competing for the gold medal. Before the bout, the American wrestler's trainer gives him a pep talk. "Don't forget all the research we've done on this Russian," says the trainer. "The guy's never lost a match because of this 'pretzel' hold he has. Whatever you do, don't let him get you in this hold! If he does, you're finished." The American wrestler nods in agreement, and the match begins. The combatants warily circle each other, looking for an opening, when all of a sudden the Russian lunges forward, grabs the American and wraps him up in the dreaded pretzel hold! A sigh of disappointment goes up from the crowd while the trainer buries his face in his hands – he knows all is lost.

Suddenly there's a scream, followed by a cheer from the crowd. The trainer raises his eyes just in time to see the Russian flying up in the air. His back hits the mat with a thud; the American weakly flops on top of him, gets the pin and wins the match.

The trainer's astounded! Rushing forward with a towel he throws it over his boy, then hisses, "How did you ever get out of that hold? No-one's ever done it before!"

"Well, I was ready to give up," the wrestler explains, "but at the last moment I opened my eyes and saw this pair of balls hanging right in front of my face! I thought I had nothing to lose, so with my last ounce of strength I stretched out my neck and chomped down on those plums just as hard as I could."

"And that worked!" says the trainer.

"Oh yes," replies the wrestler. "You'd be amazed how strong you get when you bite your own balls."

A: BUS SHELTERS.

> # A three-legged dog...
> ...walks into a wild west saloon. He sidles up to the bar and announces, *"I'm looking for the man who shot my paw."*

Doc tests oldies

The senior house doctor is doing his weekly rounds at the nursing home. As usual, he conducts a memory test with three elderly residents, asking the first lady what three times three is.

"Hmm…." thinks the old girl, "ah, I know – 274!" The doctor sighs, shakes his head and proceeds to the next woman in the line. "Can you tell me what three times three is, please?" he asks.

"Sure can!" says the lady, "Tuesday!"

The doc moves on. "Okay," he says, finally arriving at the third patient, "three times three – what's the answer?"

"Nine," comes the reply, sharp as a knife.

"Blimey!" says the doc, impressed, "how did you arrive at the answer?"

"Easy," she replies, "I just subtracted 274 from Tuesday."

The prying priest

A priest in a small village is walking down the street one evening when he hears music and laughter coming from one of the houses. He decides to knock on the door and find out what's going on.

"Hello there, Father," replies an old lady. "And how are you on this fine evening?"

"Actually I was wondering what was going on," says the reverend. "Are you having a party?"

"Yes, we are," says the biddy. "Perhaps you'd like to join in? All the young folk in the village are here playing a game."

"And what game is that?" asks the priest.

"Well," goes the lady, "all the boys get naked and so do all the girls."

"My God!" shrieks the priest. "What kind of party is this?"

"I'm not finished," explains the old bag. "Then the girls all put on blindfolds and have to go up to each boy, feel his bits and pieces and guess which boy it is."

"Stop, stop!" screams the priest. "I can't hear any more! Do you really believe that I would be involved in such an event?"

"Well actually, Father, your name has come up a few times…"

> # What qualifications do you need...
> ...to be a road sweeper? *None. You just pick it up as you go along.*

Q: WHAT CAN A LAWYER DO THAT A DUCK CAN'T?

Two-stroke penalty

A man staggers into an A&E with a golf club wrapped around his throat. Concerned, the doctor asks what happened. "Well," begins the man, "I was having a quiet round of golf with the wife when she sliced her ball into a field full of cows. We went to look for it and while I was rooting around I noticed one of these cows had something small and white in its backside. I walked over, lifted up its tail and, sure enough, there was the wife's golf ball lodged right in the middle of its arse… and that's when I made my mistake."

"What did you do?" asks the doc.

"I yelled to my wife: 'Hey! This looks like yours!'"

Birds of a feather

Two men are standing on the edge of a cliff. One has a budgie on each shoulder, the other has a parrot on one shoulder. The first jumps off the cliff and, halfway down, the budgies fly off. He hits the ground with a wet splat. Barely alive, he rolls around, groaning.

Now the second man jumps off the cliff. Halfway down the parrot flies off, so the man reaches into his jacket and pulls out a shotgun. He shoots the parrot… just before landing on the rocks with a sickening thud.

As they both lie there in pain, the first man comments: "I don't think much of this budgie jumping."

The second replies, "I don't think much of this free-fall parrot-shooting, either."

Blonde pipes up

A class of aspiring female psychiatrists attend their first lecture, on emotional extremes. "To establish some parameters," says the professor, "what is the opposite of joy?"

"Sadness," replies a brunette.

"And the opposite of depression?"

"Elation," blurts out another brunette.

"Very good. And you, young lady," he says, pointing to a blonde at the back, "what about the opposite of woe?"

"Easy," she says, "giddy up!"

A: STICK ITS BILL UP ITS ARSE.

The first day at school

Four-year-old Billy is about to start his first day at school. Just before he leaves, however, his dad goes up to him and tells him, "Right, Billy – since you are now starting school, from now on you're to speak only proper English. No more 'choo-choo train' or childish phrases like that."

Billy agrees and makes his way to school. A few hours later, the lad arrives back home to be greeted by his dad. "Hi, son! How was your first day at school?"

"Okay," Billy replies.

"Did you do anything exciting?" says his dad.

"Yes, I read a book."

"Well done!" his dad exclaims. "And what book did you read?"

"Winnie the Shit."

The sweary tots

Little Timmy and Little Bobby go to visit their grandmother in the country. They've been brought up in a fairly ill-disciplined household and are prone to swearing. Anyway, after about a solid week of cursing and swearing their grandmother can't take it any more, so she goes to see her friend Maude to get some advice.

"What can I do about them swearing?" says the grandmother.

"As far as I'm concerned there is only really one thing you can do," says Maude. "Next time they swear, just hit 'em good and hard and they won't do it again."

"I can't do that!" says grandma, shocked at the thought. "They're my grandchildren!"

"Look," says Maude, "It'll teach 'em a good lesson, mark my words." So grandma leaves and goes home. The next morning Timmy and Bobby go downstairs to have breakfast. Grandma says to Bobby, "And what would you like for breakfast?"

To which Bobby replies, "Give me some of them fucking cornflakes!" Grandma lashes out with this big swing and knocks Bobby clean out of his chair. He sits on the ground, looking shocked. Next Grandma turns to Timmy: "And what would you like for breakfast, little Timmy?" Timmy looks at his brother, then back to his grandmother, and says, "I don't know – but you can bet your sweet arse it won't be fucking cornflakes."

Patient reprimanded

A guy goes to the doctor and is confronted by the receptionist. "What's wrong?" she asks.

"It's my knob!" exclaims the bloke. The receptionist complains to the doctor and when he sees the patient he tells him not to be so specific and to stop shocking everyone in the waiting room. A few weeks go past and the guy shows up again.

"What's the problem?" asks the receptionist.

"It's my ear," says the guy.

"What's wrong with it?" she asks.

"I can't piss out of it," mumbles the man.

Q: WHAT'S THE DEFINITION OF "MAKING LOVE"?

The skiving builders

An Englishman, a Scotsman and an Irishman are on a building site when the foreman says, "I'm going off-site for an hour – anyone leaves here and they're fired!"

Naturally, the moment he's gone the Englishman says, "To hell with this – if he's off then I'm going down the boozer."

"Too right," says the Scotsman. "I'm going down the bookies."

"I'm off to see the missus," says the Irishman, and he goes home. As he opens the front door, however, he hears panting and groaning from upstairs, so he goes to investigate. As he peeks through the bedroom door, what does he see but the foreman shagging his wife, so he scampers downstairs and back to the building site. The next day at the site the foreman once again says he's going off for an hour, and that anybody leaving the site will be fired. Immediately the Englishman announces that he's sloping off to the pub and the Scotsman says he's off to the bookies but, when asked, the Irishman says that he's going to stay and get on with his work. The Englishman and Scotsman are shocked. "Why don't you go home?" asks the Englishman.

"You must be joking," says the Irishman. "I nearly got caught yesterday!"

> **How do you make your girlfriend scream... ...after an orgasm?** *Wipe your dick on the curtains.*

Lucky Linda

A man goes down for breakfast, where it's quite obvious his wife has the hump with him. He asks what's the matter. She replies, "Last night you were talking in your sleep. I want to know exactly who 'Linda' is!"

Thinking quickly, he tells her that he was dreaming of "Lucky Linda" – a horse he'd bet on and that had won him £40.

The wife seems quite happy with the explanation and he goes off to work, but when he gets home that night his wife has the hump with him once again.

"What is it now, my love?" the man enquires.

"Your horse phoned," she growls.

The big kiss

At the back of the cinema, a girl and a boy are kissing passionately – until they finally stop and come up for air. "Look," pants the boy, "I really love kissing you, but do you mind not passing me your chewing gum?"

"Oh, that's not chewing gum," replies the girl. "I've got bronchitis."

> **What did the blonde... ...get on her IQ test?** *Nail varnish.*

The nuns' interrogation

Three nuns died in a car crash and found themselves standing before the Pearly Gates. Saint Peter greeted them and said they would have to answer one question each before being admitted into the Kingdom of Heaven. Sister Mary said, "Saint Peter, I'm ready for my question." Peter consulted a heavy volume and read out, "Your question is: Who was the first man on Earth?" The nun replied, "Why, it was Adam." And the lights flashed, the bells tolled and the gates of Heaven opened. Sister Bernadette stepped forward for her question and Peter intoned, "Who was the first woman on Earth?" "Eve," the nun replied. And the lights flashed, the bells tolled and the gates of Heaven opened. Mother Superior stepped forward and said, "I'm ready, Saint Peter!" Peter turned to his book for a third time, before reading out, "And what was the first thing Eve said to Adam?" The nun was shocked. "My goodness," she said, "that's a hard one." And the lights flashed, the bells tolled and the gates of Heaven opened.

What do you call...
...a ferret on ecstasy....
Madferret.

The lucky punter

A bloke is walking along the street and he finds a little oil lamp in the gutter. So he picks it up, gives it a rub and out pops a genie. "I grant you one wish," the genie says. The bloke thinks for a while, and eventually requests that he be incredibly lucky for the day. "So be it!" says the genie, and disappears in a puff of smoke. So the man's walking along the road, wishing he had some cash so he could go down to the bookies to test the theory out, when all of a sudden he sees a spanking new £50 note in the gutter. "How lucky," he says to himself as he sets off for the bookies. Having placed the whole £50 on the nose on a 400-1 long-shot, he waits for the race. Eventually his horse comes in second. What a shame. All of a sudden

Q: WHAT CAN YOU SAY TO A MAN WHO'S JUST HAD SEX?

What do men with two left feet... ...wear on the beach? *Flip-flips.*

giving her a good seeing to in the pub toilets. "How lucky," he thinks to himself. However, after a couple of minutes he stops. "Look, I'm sorry," he says, "I know it's a religious thing, but I can't take my eyes off that red dot on your forehead. It's ruining my concentration." "Don't worry," she says, "it's just a bit of paint – scratch it off." So he scratches at the spot. "Bugger me, I've won a car!"

there's an announcement – there has been a steward's enquiry and the winner has been disqualified, making his horse the winner! "How lucky," he thinks to himself. He decides to celebrate with a drink and wanders off to his local. As he walks through the door hundreds of lights start flashing and a siren sounds. "Congratulations, sir!" says the landlord. "You're our one-millionth customer – free drinks for you all night!" "How lucky," he thinks to himself. So he sits down with his mates and tells them about the day's events. None of them believe him, so they set a challenge. The Indian barmaid is sexy as hell – but none of them has managed to bed her yet. That is his challenge. So he goes up to the Indian barmaid and starts chatting. They're getting on superbly, when the next thing he knows he's

The freezer of punishment

A man buys a parrot for his kids, but the bird is simply obnoxious. He uses bad language and no-one can handle it without getting pinched, until finally one day when the bird insults the man's wife. He grabs the parrot and tosses it cursing and flapping into the freezer, slamming the door behind it.

After a few seconds, all goes quiet. The man opens the door and the parrot meekly walks out. "I realise I've offended you and I'm sorry and humbly beg your forgiveness," says the potty-mouthed pet.

The man is touched.

"That's okay," he says. You're forgiven."

"Good" says the parrot. "Now, if I might ask: what did the chicken do?"

Man of God offers solace

Mary pulls aside the Father following his Sunday morning service. She's in tears, and the priest is worried, "What could possibly be bothering you, Mary my dear?"

"Oh, Father," sobs Mary, " I've terrible news – my husband passed away last night!"

"Oh sweet Jesus, Mary," says the Father, "that's terrible! Tell me, Mary, did he have any last requests?"

"That he did, Father," replies Mary, "that he did… he screamed, 'Please Mary, put down that damn gun!'"

A: ANYTHING YOU LIKE – HE'S ASLEEP.

Two cannibals were eating a clown...

...when one said to the other, *"Here – does this taste funny to you?"*

The voodoo dick

A businessman was going on a long trip abroad so thought he'd get his wife something to keep her occupied while he was gone. He went to a sex shop and explained the situation to the man behind the counter. "Well, sir, I don't usually mention this, but there is the 'voodoo dick'." The man reached under the counter and pulled out an ornate wooden box. He opened it, and there lay a very ordinary-looking dildo. The man pointed to a door and said, "Voodoo dick, the door." The voodoo dick rose out of its box, darted over to the door, and started screwing the keyhole. The whole door shook with the vibrations and a crack developed down the middle. The man said, "Voodoo dick, get back in your box!" The voodoo dick stopped and floated back to its box. "I'll take it!" said the businessman. When he gave it to his wife he explained that it was a special dildo and that to use it, all she had to do was say, "Voodoo dick, my pussy." Then he left for his trip. After he'd been gone a few days, the wife found herself unbearably horny, so she got the voodoo dick out and said, "Voodoo dick, my pussy!" The voodoo dick shot to her crotch and started pumping. It was like nothing she'd ever experienced before. After three orgasms, however, she decided she'd had enough and tried to pull it out – but it was stuck. Her husband had forgotten to tell her how to shut it off, so she drove to the hospital to see if they could help. On the way,

Why did God...

...let women have orgasms? *It gives them something else to moan about.*

another orgasm nearly made her swerve off the road, and she was pulled over by a policeman. He demanded her licence, then asked how much she'd had to drink. She explained she hadn't been drinking, but that a voodoo dick was stuck in her fanny. The officer said, "Yeah, right. Voodoo dick, my arse."

Canine contraceptives

Two dogs, walking down the road. One dog says, "Do you use a condom when you're making love?" The other dog replies, "Durex." "No," says dog number one. "I asked you first."

 Q: WHAT'S BLACK AND WHITE AND EATS LIKE A HORSE?

The shipwreck survivor

A cruise liner sinks and the sole survivor finds himself on a deserted island. For the next four months he eats nothing but bananas and drinks coconut milk. One day he sees a rowboat, and in it is the most gorgeous woman he's ever seen. "How did you get here?" gasps the man. "I rowed from the other side of the island," says the woman. "I washed up there when my ship sank."

"Amazing," says the man. "You were lucky to have a rowboat wash up with you!"

"The rowboat didn't wash up," says the woman. "I made it from gum branches, palm branches and a eucalyptus."

"But," stutters the man, "you had no tools."

"Oh, that was no problem," replies the woman. "The island is littered with an alluvial rock. When I fired it to a certain temperature in my kiln, it melted into ductile iron. I used that to make tools. Why don't we row over to my place now?" says the woman. After a journey of a few minutes, she docks the boat at a small wharf. In front of them is an exquisite bungalow. The man can only stare, dumbstruck.

"Would you like a drink?" asks the woman.

"I'm sick of coconut milk," mutters the man. "Don't be silly!" the woman replies. "I have a still. How about a piña colada?"

Trying to hide his amazement, the man accepts, and they sit down to talk. After they've exchanged stories, the woman announces, "I'm going to slip into something comfortable. Would you like to take a shower and shave?" The man goes into the bathroom and finds a razor made from bone and cowry shells. He scrapes off his beard and goes back to the living room, where the woman is wearing nothing but vines and smelling faintly of gardenias. She beckons him to sit down next to her. "Tell me," she whispers, slithering closer, "we've been out here for a very long time. You've been lonely. I've been lonely. There's something I'm sure you feel like doing right now, something you've been longing for all these months…" She stares into his eyes.

"You mean…?" he stutters, "…you mean I can check my e-mail from here?"

A: A ZEBRA.

The customer's always right

A woman goes into a US sporting goods store to buy a rifle. "It's for my husband," she tells the clerk.

"Did he tell you what gauge to get?" asks the clerk.

"Are you kidding?" she says. "He doesn't even know that I'm going to shoot him!"

Explorers amazed

Paddy and Murphy are strolling through the jungle by a riverbank when they spy a crocodile with a man's head protruding from its mouth.

Paddy turns to Murphy and says, "Would you look at that flash twat in his Lacoste sleeping bag…"

The nervous parachutist

A young man joined the army and signed up for paratrooper training, and finally went to take his first jump from an aeroplane. The next day, he phoned his father to tell him what had happened.

"So, did you jump?" the father asked.

"Well, we got up in the plane, and the Sergeant opened the door and asked for volunteers. About a dozen men got up and just leapt out the aircraft!"

"Is that when you jumped?" asked the father.

"Um, not yet. Then the Sergeant started to grab the remaining men one at a time and threw them out the door."

"Did you jump then?" asked the father.

"I'm getting to that," said the youngster. "I was the last man left on the plane and told the Sergeant I was too scared to jump. He told me to leap out of the plane or he'd kick my arse."

"So, did you jump?"

"Not then. I grabbed onto the door and refused to go, so he called over the Jump Master – this great big guy, must have been six-foot five and 17 stone. He said to me, 'Boy, are you going to jump or not?' I said, 'No, Sir. I'm too scared.' So the Jump Master pulled down his zip and took his penis out. I swear, it was ten inches long! He said, 'Boy, either you jump out of that door, or I'm sticking this up your arse.'"

"So, did you jump?" asked the father.

"Well, a little, at first."

Q: WHAT DO YOU CALL AN IRISH LESBIAN?

Thanks, waitress

A couple are dining in a restaurant when the man suddenly slides under the table. A waitress, noticing that the woman is glancing nonchalantly around the room, wanders over to check that there's no funny business going on.

"Excuse me, madam," she smarms, "but I think your husband has just slid under the table."

"No he hasn't," the woman replies. "As a matter of fact, he's just walked in."

Wild west watches

One day in the old west, a rancher was riding along, checking the fence around his property. After a while he came across an Indian, lying in the dirt, completely naked and with a huge erection. "What the hell are you doing?" asked the rancher. "I'm telling the time," said the redskin. He looked at the shadow cast by his penis and said, "It's one o'clock."

The rancher kept on riding until, after an hour, he came across another Indian, lying in the dirt completely naked, with a huge hard-on. "Are you telling the time, too?" asked the rancher.

"Sure am," said the Indian. Then he looked at the shadow cast by his penis and said, "It's two o'clock."

The rancher rode on for another hour until he came to a third Indian, lying in the dirt completely naked and masturbating vigorously.

"Those other two Indians were telling the time," said the rancher. "Why the hell are you whacking off like that?"

"I'm winding my watch," the brave replied.

The Lottery winner

A man wins the Lottery and decides to buy himself a top-of-the-range superbike. The shop's owner warns him to coat the bike in Vaseline every time it looks like raining.

That night he goes and picks his girlfriend up on his new toy and heads over to her parents' house for the first time. As they arrive, she explains to him that when they have dinner, he shouldn't talk. "It's a family tradition," she tells him. "If you say anything, you'll have to do the pots."

As the girlfriend warned, the family sit down for dinner without anyone saying a word. So the man decides to take advantage of the situation by groping his girlfriend's tits. Not a sound comes from anyone.

So he decides to shag his bird on the table – still, not a word. He then proceeds to do his girlfriend's mum over the table – still, amazingly, not a word.

Suddenly he notices spots of rain on the kitchen window and remembers his precious motorbike, so he reaches into his pocket and gets out the Vaseline, at which point his girlfriend's dad leaps up and shouts, "Okay, I'll do the pots."

What do you call...

...two skunks having a 69? *Odour eaters.*

A: GAELIC.

How do you make...
...a cat go woof?
Cover it in petrol.

Skill demonstrated

A young man visits a talent scout, claiming he has an unbelievable act. "Okay then," says the scout, "show me what you can do."

With that, the man pulls a claw hammer from his pocket and chows it down within seconds – wood, metal, the lot.

"Bravo!" says the talent scout, clapping wildly and rising to his feet. "Do you do this professionally?"

"Oh no," replies the man, "I'm an 'ammer chewer."

Bunda!

While out on an expedition, three explorers get caught by a race of brutal savages. The chief goes up to the first explorer and makes him a simple offer. "Choose," says the chief. "Death or *bunda*?" The first explorer thinks about this and decides that anything has to be better than death, so he chooses *bunda*. The chief turns to his followers, shouts, "*Bunda!*" and cuts the explorer loose, telling him to run.

The first explorer legs it, hotly pursued by a group of whooping, hollering savages. Moments later, however, he is caught, dragged into some bushes and brutally buggered in every orifice. The chief turns to the second explorer and asks, "Death or *bunda*?"

The second explorer, reckoning he can make a better job of escaping, chooses *bunda*. Again, the chief turns to his followers, shouts, "*Bunda!*" cuts the explorer loose and tells him to run. The second explorer runs even quicker than the first, but eventually he too is caught by the savages and subjected to the most vile of buggerings. Finally, the chief turns to the third explorer and asks, "Death or *bunda*?" The guy thinks about what happened to his colleagues and, taking a deep breath, chooses death. The chief stares at him with a look of pity in his eyes, turns to his followers and shouts, "Death! By *bunda*!"

An inspector calls

A TV licence inspector knocks at the door as the owner's hurriedly on her way out. "Just here to check your licence, madam," he politely asks.

"I'm terribly late already," explains the woman, "come back at three and see my husband – tell him it's behind the clock on the mantelpiece."

At three sharp, the inspector returns. "Hello, sir, I'm here to see your television licence."

"I'm awfully sorry," replies the man, "I haven't a clue where it is."

"No problem," says the inspector, "it's behind the clock on the mantelpiece…"

"Sweet Jesus," replies the man, "I knew your equipment was good, but not that bloody good!"

Q: WHY ARE MEN LIKE PUBLIC TOILETS?

> ## What do Americans use...
> ### ...as contraception?
> ## *Their personalities.*

Emergency service

Two hunters are out in the woods when one suddenly cries out and falls to the ground. He doesn't appear to be breathing and his eyes are rolled back in his head, so the friend panics and telephones 999 on his mobile.

"My friend is dead!" he gasps to the operator. "What can I do?"

The operator, speaking in a soothing voice, calms him

> ## What's the difference...
> ## ...between toast and women?
> ## *You can make soldiers out of toast.*

down. "Just take it easy. I can help. First, let's make sure he's dead."

The line goes silent for a moment, and there's a loud bang before the man comes back on the line.

"Okay," he says breathlessly, "now what?"

The priest's bath

It was time for Father John's Saturday night bath. A young sister, Jane, had prepared the bathwater and towels just the way the old nun instructed. Sister Jane

was also told firstly, not to look at Father John's nakedness if she could help it; secondly, do whatever he told her to do; and thirdly, to pray.

The next morning the old nun asked Sister Jane how the bath went. "Oh, sister," said the young nun dreamily. "I've been saved."

"Saved? And how did that fine thing come about?" asked the old nun.

"Well, while Father John was soaking in the tub, he asked me to wash him. While I was washing him he guided my hand down between his legs, where he said the Lord keeps the key to Heaven!"

"Did he now," said the old nun, evenly.

Sister Jane continued, "And Father John said that if the key to Heaven fit my lock, the portals of Heaven would be opened to me and I would be assured of salvation and eternal peace. And then Father John guided his key to Heaven into my lock."

"Is that a fact?" said the senior nun, even more evenly.

"At first it hurt terribly, but Father John said the pathway to salvation was often painful and that the glory of God would soon swell my heart with ecstasy. And it did! It felt so good being saved!"

"That wicked old devil," said the old nun. "He told me it was Gabriel's Horn, and I've been blowing it for 40 years…"

Why do women... ...have small feet?
To get closer to the oven.

Court of appeal
A man appears in court requesting a divorce. After reviewing the papers, the judge turns to him. "Please tell me why I should grant this," he asks.

"Because," the man replies, "we live in a two-storey house."

The judge looks at him sternly. "What kind of a reason is that? What's the big deal about a two-storey house?"

"Well, your honour," the man answers, "one story is 'I have a headache,' and the other story is 'It's that time of the month.'"

Elevator etiquette
A man is in the back of a crowded elevator when he yells, "Ballroom, please!" The lady in front of him turns around and says, "Sorry – I didn't know I was crowding you."

Virgin gets a shock
A virgin gets married to a man who is supposed to be rather well endowed. On the first night of their honeymoon she confesses her fears to her new husband, who tells her that he'll get round the situation by showing her his dick bit by bit. So the wife is lying in bed when she sees three inches of dick come round the door. "Are you nervous yet?" asks her husband.

"No, I'm okay," she replies. Another six inches of dick comes around the door. "Are you still okay?" he asks. "Yes," she replies. A further foot comes around the door. "I'm not nervous," she calls. "Okay," her husband replies. "I'm coming up the stairs."

Loan repaid
Chris goes to see his friend Tony. Tony's wife Sara answers the door and says that Tony has gone shopping, but Chris can wait if he wants. After a few minutes Chris says, "Sara, you have the greatest breasts I've ever seen. I'd give you £100 if I could just see one." Sara thinks about this for a minute and figures what the hell – 100 quid for a flash! So she opens her robe and shows a nork. Chris politely thanks her, pulls two £50 notes from his pocket and throws them on the table. Then Chris says, "I've just got to see the both of them – I'll give you another 100 notes if I could see the both of them together." Sara thinks, "For £100?" then opens her robe and gives Chris a long look. He throws another £100 on the table, then says he can't wait any longer for Tony and leaves. A while later Tony arrives home. "Your weird friend Chris came over," his wife tells him.

"Great," says Tony. "Did he leave the £200 he owes me?"

Did you hear about... ...the paraplegic juggler?
He dropped all the paraplegics.

Q: WHAT'S THE BEST THING ABOUT HAVING ALZHEIMER'S?

Towel therapy

After marrying a younger woman, a middle-aged man finds that no matter what he does in the sack, she never achieves orgasm. So he visits his doctor for advice. "Maybe fantasy is the solution," says the doctor. "Why not hire a strapping young man and, while you two are making love, have him wave a towel over you?" The doctor smiles. "Make sure he's totally naked – that way your wife can fantasise her way to a full-blown orgasm." Optimistic, he returns home and hires a handsome young escort. But it's no use: even when the stud stands naked, waving the towel, the wife remains unsatisfied. Perplexed, the man returns to his doctor. "Try reversing it for a while," says the quack. "Have the young man make love to your wife and you wave the towel over them." And so he returns home to try again – this time, waving the towel as the same escort pumps away enthusiastically. Soon the wife has an enormous, screaming orgasm. Smiling, the husband drops the towel and taps the young man on the shoulder. "You see?" he shouts triumphantly. "That's how you wave a bloody towel."

Gramps treats kids

An old man takes his two grandchildren to see the new *Scooby-Doo* film. When he returns home, his wife asks if he enjoyed himself.
"Well," he starts, "if it wasn't for those pesky kids…!"

Blind ambition

A blind man walks into a supermarket. He grabs his guide dog by the tail and swings it around his head.
"What the hell do you think you're doing?" shouts a sales assistant.
"Having a look round," replies the blind man.

A: YOU GET TO MEET NEW PEOPLE EVERY DAY.

What has an old woman got... ...between her tits that a young woman hasn't? *Her belly button.*

Sexual economics

A couple in their late sixties make an appointment to see a sex therapist, and ask him if they can have sex while he watches. Puzzled, the doctor nevertheless agrees – and sits quietly while the elderly lovers get down to it. After a screaming climax, the physician nods solemnly. "In my professional opinion," he says, "there's nothing wrong with the way you have intercourse." Happy, the couple pay the £50 fee and leave – only to return the next week and repeat the exercise. This continues for several weeks, and each time the doctor has to conclude that no matter what the position, the paramour pensioners are perfectly adequate at shagging. Finally, the doctor himself becomes curious. "Just exactly what are you trying to find out?" he asks. "Nothing," says the old man, "but she's married and we can't go to her house. I'm married and we can't go to mine."
"So why come to me?" says the doctor.
The old man grins. "Well," he beams, "the Holiday Inn charges £90. The Hilton charges £108. We do it here for £50 – and I get £43 back from Bupa."

Patient request worries staff

A man lies on his hospital bed, desperately ill with an oxygen mask covering his mouth. A young nurse arrives to sponge his face and hands. "Nurse," he mumbles, "are my testicles black?" Embarrassed, the young nurse explains how she's only there to wash him, and carries on about her business.
"Please nurse," pleads the man, again, "I have to know, are my testicles black?" Again the nurse refuses to check, but duly concerned she summons the ward sister to see what the problem is. "Sister," the man mumbles, clearly in pain, "all I want to know is – are my testicles black?" With that, the ward sister whips off the sheets, strips him and has a good poke around his clockweights. Nothing. "There's absolutely nothing wrong with those," she yells at the man, "now please leave us to do our job!"
"For Christ's sake," shouts the man, pulling away the oxygen mask, "I couldn't give a hoot about my bollocks – I want to know if my test results are back!"

What did the leper... ...say to his mother while riding his bike? *"Look mum, no hands!"*

A man walks into a bar...

...with a steering wheel in his underpants. The barman asks, "Is that painful?" The man replies, "It's driving me nuts!"

The lucky frog

A man is playing a practice round of golf, when he notices a frog sitting next to the green. Thinking nothing of it, he takes out a six iron to play his shot when he hears: "Ribbit. Nine iron."

The man looks around. There's no-one in sight, so he lines up his shot once more. "Ribbit. Nine iron." He gives the frog a long look and, putting his other club away, grabs the nine iron. Thwack! He puts the ball ten inches from the hole! "You must be a lucky frog," he tells the frog.

"Ribbit. Lucky frog," the creature replies.

The man picks the frog up and carries him to the next hole. "What do you think, little fella?" he asks.

"Ribbit. Three wood," comes the reply.

The man takes out a three wood, and boom! Hole in one. Two hours later, he's played the best round of golf in his life, so he decides to take the frog to Las Vegas. As soon as the plane touches down the frog pipes up, "Ribbit. Roulette." As the wheel spins, the frog's there again: "Ribbit. $3,000, black six." The man plonks all his money down. Result! Black six! The man takes his winnings and checks into the best room in the hotel. He says to the frog, "I don't know how to repay you."

"Ribbit. Kiss me," the frog replies. The man puckers up – why not, after all the frog's done for him? And with that kiss, the frog turns into a gorgeous 15-year-old girl.

"And that, Your Honour, is how she ended up in my room."

IT'S CALLED GO AND WASH.

> **What are the three worst things ...**
> **...about being an egg?**
> **You only get laid once, it takes ten minutes to go hard and the only bird to sit on your face is your mum.**

Weevil rivalry

Two boll-weevils grew up in North Carolina. Eventually, one upped and left for Hollywood where it became a famous actor. The other stayed behind, tending to the cotton fields, never amounting to much. This second one, naturally, became known as the lesser of two weevils.

Jim's Nails

A man named Jim owned a small company which manufactured nails. One night he bumped into his old schoolmate, Bob. They got talking and Bob asked Jim what he was doing. "I own my own nail manufacturing company, called Jim's Nails," he said. "What about you?" "Oh, I make adverts for TV," said Bob. "Tell you what, since we were friends at school I'll make you an advert for free." So a few days later, Bob phoned him to say that his advert would be on in the middle of *Coronation Street*.

Jim waited for his spot, only to find that the "advert" was simply a picture of Jesus nailed to a cross with the caption "Use Jim's Nails" written in large letters. Being a good Catholic, Jim was outraged. He phoned Bob up and asked him what the hell he thought he was doing. Bob apologised profusely, and offered to shoot another spot to make it up to his old school buddy. A few days later, in the middle of *The Bill*, the new ad came on: Jesus was running through the desert with sweat pouring down his brow, obviously running for his life. The camera panned out to reveal two Roman guards about 100 yards behind Jesus, chasing after him. The camera zoomed in on the guards just as one said to the other, "I told you we should have used Jim's Nails."

Second opinion

One day a bloke goes into the doctor's and says, "Doc, I get these splitting headaches. They've ruined my sex life! What do you recommend?" So the doctor says, "There's only one answer, I'm afraid. You'll have to have your penis amputated." Knowing that he has to get rid of the headaches, the man reluctantly agrees – so a week later he goes into hospital for the op. After the operation he feels he should celebrate by buying himself a new suit. He makes his way to the tailor's for his new garments. Whilst the tailor measures his inside leg he asks, "Which side does your penis hang, sir?" Worried, the man says: "Does it really matter?" "Well, yes," says the tailor, "if you hang it over the wrong side you get these splitting headaches."

Q: WHAT DID CINDERELLA DO WHEN SHE GOT TO THE BALL?

What goes... ..."Oooooo"? A cow with no lips.

Alien invasion thwarted

Two aliens landed in the Arizona desert near an abandoned gas station. They approached one of the petrol pumps, and one of them said to it, "Greetings, Earthling. We come in peace. Take us to your leader."

The petrol pump, of course, didn't respond. The alien repeated the greeting. Again, no response. The alien, annoyed by what he perceived to be the petrol pump's haughty attitude, drew his ray gun and said impatiently, "Earthling, how dare you ignore us in this way! Take us to your leader or I will fire!"

The other alien shouted to his comrade, "No, you mustn't anger him!" but before he finished his warning, the first alien fired. There was a huge explosion that blew both of them 200 yards into the desert, where they landed in a heap. When they finally regained consciousness, the one who fired turned to the other one and said, "What a ferocious creature. It nearly killed us! But how did you know he was so dangerous?"

The other alien answered, "If there's one thing I've learned during all my travels through the galaxy, it's that if a guy has a penis he can wrap around himself twice and then stick into his own ear, don't mess with him!"

A rural Christmas

Two farmers were leaning over a fence discussing Christmas. The first farmer said that he bought his wife a fur coat and a Mercedes for the festive season.

The second farmer asked why he bought her such expensive presents. The first farmer replied that if she didn't like the coat, she could drive in the Mercedes to take it back. The second farmer nodded his head, understanding the reasoning behind the answer. The first farmer then asked the second what he got his wife for Christmas. He replied that he bought his wife a pair of slippers and a vibrator. "Why that combination?" asked the first farmer.

"Well," said the second, "if she didn't like the slippers she could go fuck herself."

Customer complaint

A middle-aged woman walks into a sex shop and asks the shop owner, "D-d-do you s-s-sell vibrators?"

"Yes madam, we do," replies the man.

"D-d-do you s-s-sell them th-this big?" the woman asks, holding her hands about 12 inches apart.

"Yes – we sell them that big."

"D-d-do you s-s-sell them th-this w-wide?" the woman asks, holding her hands about four inches apart.

"Yes, we sell them that wide."

"D-d-do you ha-have them with b-batteries?"

"Yes we do."

"W-well, how the f-f-fuck do you t-t-turn them off?!"

A: SHE CHOKED.

What have parsley... ...and pubic hair got in common? *You just push it to the side and carry on eating.*

Prostitute inflation

Three prostitutes once lived together: a grandmother, mother and daughter. One night the daughter came home looking very upset. "How did you get on tonight, dear?" asked her mother. "Not too good," replied the daughter. "I only got £20 for a blow job." "Wow!" said the mother, "in my day we gave a blow job for 50p!" "Good God!" said the grandmother. "In my day we were just glad to get something warm in our stomachs."

Rewarding ramble

A man arrives back from a long business trip and finds that his son has a brand new £500 mountain bike. "How did you get that, son?" "By hiking," replies the boy. "Hiking?" asks his old man. "That's right," says the boy. "Every night while you were away, your boss came over and mum gave me £20 to take a hike."

In-law comes a cropper

A big-game hunter is on safari with his wife and mother-in-law. One night, his wife wakes up to discover her mother is gone, so wakes her husband and insists they search for the old girl. Rifle in hand, he wanders to the edge of the camp where – shock horror – the mother-in-law is backed up against a tree with a huge lion inching towards her. "Oh no," screams the wife, "what are we going to do?" "Nothing," replies her husband, "the lion got himself into this mess, let him get out of it."

Catholic logic

Two Irishmen were digging a ditch opposite a brothel when they saw a rabbi enter its front door. "Will you look at that?" the first ditch-digger said. "What's our world comin' to when men of the cloth are visitin' such places?" A short time later, a Protestant minister walked up to the door and slipped inside. "Do you believe that?" the same workman exclaimed. "Why, 'tis no wonder the young people today are so confused, what with the example clergymen set for them." Another hour went by, and the men watched as a Catholic priest quickly entered the whorehouse. "Ah, what a pity," the digger said. "One of the poor lasses must be ill."

What have Posh Spice... ...and Alan Shearer got in common? *They're both fucking good footballers.*

Q: WHY ARE GIRLS LIKE PIANOS?

Driver carries no cash

One dismal rainy night, a taxi driver spots an arm waving from the shadows of an alley. Even before he rolls to a stop at the curb, a figure leaps into the cab and slams the door. Checking his mirror as he pulls away, the cabbie is startled to see a dripping wet, naked woman sitting in the back seat. "Er, where to?" he stammers. "The station," answers the woman.

"You got it," he nods, taking another long glance in the mirror. Looking up, the woman catches him staring. "Just what the hell are you looking at, driver?" The driver coughs politely. "Well, I'd just noticed that you were completely naked." "So?"

"I was just wondering how you'll pay your fare." Nodding slowly, the woman spreads her legs and puts her feet up on the front seat headrests. She smiles at the driver. "Does this answer your question?"

"Bloody hell," cries the cabbie, still staring in the mirror. "Got anything smaller?"

War wounds

Two elderly gents are taking a leak in a public toilet when one notices the other gent is pissing two streams. "What the hell is that?" he asks. "War wound," replies the other. "I took a revolver bullet in the penis in North Africa, which left a hole."

"Me too," says the first – showing he's pissing with three streams. "War wound, Germany. A high-powered rifle round in the penis – left me with two holes."

At this point, a young lad stands between them – and squirts 12 streams of amber onto the porcelain.

"My God," exclaims the second veteran, "did you get that from a machine gun?"

"No mate," says the youngster, incredulously. "My zip's stuck."

Third time unlucky

While admiring the view from her flat on the 20th floor of an apartment building, a young woman slips and falls out of the window. Luckily, she's caught by the ankle a few floors down by a man who happens to be out on his balcony. "Thank the Lord you were there!" gasps the young woman.

The man simply asks, "Do you suck?"

"No!" says the horrified young woman. The man immediately drops her.

But she only falls a couple more floors when she's once again caught by a man out on his balcony. "Thank you!" she gasps. The man simply asks, "Do you fuck?"

"No!" she exclaims, and he lets her go.

As she falls, she prays for one last chance. And lo and behold, a third man catches her from his balcony. Quickly she blurts out, "I suck, I fuck!"

"Slut," he says, and drops her.

Q: WHAT DO YOU CALL A SMART BLONDE?

Hooker stressed

Fearing she might be a haemophiliac, a prostitute visits her GP. "It's awful," she says, "every time I get even a small cut, it takes days for the bleeding to stop."

"Hmmm," replies the physician, scribbling down notes, "and roughly how much do you lose when you get your period?"

The woman thinks for a moment. "About a grand…"

Gramps tries luck

A young man pays his grandparents an impromptu visit. Pulling into the driveway, he's flabbergasted to see his ageing grandfather shivering in a rocking chair on the porch, naked from the waist down. "What are you doing?" he shouts but the old man doesn't answer.

"Gramps," the young man perseveres, "why are you sat out here with nothing on down below?"

Slowly, the old man turns his head to greet his grandson. "Last week I sat out here without my shirt on and got a stiff neck," he wheezes. "This is your grandmother's idea…"

The stranded businessman

A businessman's car broke down on a country lane, so he walked to a nearby farmhouse. When the farmer answered he said, "May I use your phone? My car has broken down about a mile down the road."

"I'm afraid we don't have one, but I could give you a tow to town in the morning and you can stay here the night," the farmer offered.

When it came to bedtime the farmer admitted they only had one bed, so they all went to bed, with the businessman lying in the middle. After a while the businessman got a huge erection. The wife turned to the businessman and said: "Listen, if you want to sleep with me, pull a hair out of my husband's arse and see if he moves. If he doesn't, then he's asleep."

So the businessman teased a hair out of the farmer's arse. The old boy didn't move – so he shagged the wife.

Half an hour later, the businessman got another erection. Pleased with her last shag, the wife told the businessman to pull another hair out. Discovering that the farmer was still asleep, they went at it again.

Half an hour later, the businessman got another hard-on. This time, when he pulled a hair out of the farmer's arse, the old boy turned to him and said, "Look, I don't mind you shagging my wife, but do you have to use my arse as a scoreboard?"

What do you call…
…a breakdancer with no arms or legs?
Clever dick.

> ## What's the difference...
> ...between a 16-stone woman and a 16-year-old girl?
> *One is trying to diet...*

Checkout number three, please!

A man was in a really long queue at the supermarket checkout. After 15 minutes of waiting he finally reached the checkout girl – and only then remembered that he had a hot date that night. Not wanting to line up again, he said to the girl: "I meant to buy some condoms, er, but I forgot…"

"Do you know what size you are?" asked the girl.

"No."

"Okay then – drop your pants and I'll tell you what size you are."

Not being the shy type, the man duly dropped his trousers. The girl had a quick feel with her hand then said into the microphone, "One packet of large condoms to checkout three, please."

The man then pulled up his trousers, the condoms were brought to him, he paid the bill and went on his way. The next customer was a man who thought he'd like to have this nice girl fondling his prick – so said the same thing to her. A similar course of events duly took place, only this time after having a feel she said, "One packet of medium-sized condoms to checkout three, please." The condoms were duly brought to him; he paid the bill and went on his way.

Also watching this course of events was a 15-year-old boy, who decided to try the same routine. "I'd like to buy some condoms please, but I forgot…" he said to the poor sales girl.

"Do you know what size you are?"

"No."

"Okay, I'll check… mop and bucket to aisle three please."

Breaking it gently

A middle-aged couple win a holiday in a prize draw, but are dismayed to find it's for just one person. "If anyone deserves this holiday," says the husband, "it's you." Tearfully grateful, the wife accepts. A few days later, she phones home to check everything is okay.

"The weather's bad," says her husband, "but I'm eating well. Oh – and your cat's dead."

Predictably, his wife is beside herself with grief. "That's terrible," she blubs. "Why did you break the news so suddenly?"

"What do you mean?" says her husband.

"I don't know," she laments, "Er… you could have said the cat's stuck on the roof. Then tomorrow say the fire brigade was trying to get it down. Then the next day say the fireman dropped her, and she's fighting for her life at the vet's. Then, on my last day, tell me she died peacefully in her sleep."

"I see," replies her husband. "Well, you try to enjoy the rest of your holiday."

So the wife rings off, and tries to cheer herself up. The next day, she phones again to check in with hubby. "So how's everything today?" she asks.

"Well," says her husband, sighing. "Your mum's stuck on the roof…"

Q: WHAT'S GOT 75 BALLS AND SCREWS OLD LADIES?

A man walks into a bar...

...with a meat and potato pie on his head. The barman, bemused by this fellow's taste in headgear, says to him, "Why have you got a meat and potato pie on your head?"
"I always wear a meat and potato pie on my head on a Tuesday," the man replies.
"But it's only Monday today!" the barman explains.
"Shit!" says the man. "I must look like a right dickhead."

Old man scolds

Murray was sat on a bench chomping down one chocolate bar after another. After the sixth bar, the old man sat on the bench opposite wandered over.
"Hello, son," he said, "you know that eating all that chocolate isn't very good for you at all? It'll give you spots, rot your teeth and make you fat as a pig."
Murray stopped chewing. "My grandfather lived to be 107 years old," he said.
"Oh?" replied the man. "And did he eat six choccy bars one after the other?"
"No, he didn't," replied Murray. "He minded his own bloody business."

Heavenly transport

When three men go to Heaven, St Peter says to them, "How many times have you been unfaithful to your wives?"
The first man says three times, so Peter decrees he must travel round Heaven in a Fiesta. The second man says five times, so Peter makes him travel round Heaven in a Lada.
The third bloke has never been unfaithful, so Peter says, "Well done! You get to drive a Rolls-Royce in Heaven."
A while later Peter comes across the man in the Rolls at the side of the road, crying. "What's the matter?" he asks. "You have a beautiful car!"

"I know," says the man, "but I just saw my wife go past on a skateboard."

A step too far

A voluptuous woman goes to a gynaecologist, who tells her to undress at once. After she's disrobed, he begins to stroke her thigh. As he does this he says to the woman, "Do you know what I'm doing?"
"Yes," she says, "you're checking for any abrasions or dermatological abnormalities."
"That is correct," says the lecherous doctor. He then begins to fondle her breasts. "Do you know what I'm doing now?" he asks.
"Yes," says the woman, "you're checking for any lumps or breast cancer."
"That's right," replies the doctor. He then begins to have sexual intercourse with the woman. He says, "Do you know what I'm doing now?"
"Yes," she says. "You're getting herpes."

What does a blonde...

...put behind her ears to make her more attractive? *Her ankles.*

A: BINGO.

Think about it...
What does DNA stand for?
National Dyslexic Association.

Antique valued

A man drags a huge box to *Antiques Roadshow*, and after a long wait he's finally ushered towards an expert. "Where did you get this, then?" asks the ageing know-it-all behind the desk.

"It's been in my loft for 40 years," replies the man. "I assume it must be some sort of heirloom."

"I see," says the expert, looking it over. "Tell me, do you have it insured?"

"I don't," says the man, thinking his luck must be in, "should I?"

"Absolutely," insists the expert, "it's your sodding water tank."

At the nudist camp

A family are on holiday at a nudist camp. Walking around, the little boy looks at all the different-sized dicks on display. He asks his dad, "Why are those men's willies all different sizes?"

His dad replies, "Well, if you have a small dick, you are unintelligent; but if you have a big one you're brainy."

Later on the dad asks his son, "Where's your mother?"

"She's speaking to that man over there," says the little angel, "and he's getting smarter all the time."

President visits

President Bush is visiting a school where a class is discussing words and their meanings. The teacher asks Dubya if he would like to lead a discussion on the word "tragedy". Bush asks if anyone can give him an example of a tragedy, and a boy stands up.

"If my best friend was playing in the street and a car ran him over, that would be a tragedy."

"No," says Bush, "that would be an accident, son."

A little girl then raises her hand, "If a school bus carrying 20 children drove off a cliff, killing everyone, that would be a tragedy."

"I'm afraid not, missy," explains the President, "that would be a great loss."

The room goes quiet. Finally, after an embarrassing silence, way at the back of the room a small boy raises his hand. "If Air Force One, carrying you and Mrs Bush, were struck by a missile and blown to smithereens by a terrorist, that would be a tragedy."

"Fantastic," says Bush, "and can you tell me why that would be a tragedy, son?"

"Well," says the boy, "because it wouldn't be an accident, and it certainly wouldn't be a great loss."

What do you call...
...a judge with no thumbs?
Justice Fingers.

Q: WHAT ARE THE THREE WORDS YOU DON'T WANT TO HEAR

The offended waitress

A man is sitting in a restaurant, waiting to order. A stunning waitress with a plunging neckline shimmies over, her tiny skirt revealing the finest pair of legs. She smiles, her huge breasts vying for freedom from her top. "Would you like to order, sir?" she asks.

The man spies an opportunity – he's single, she's probably single… what's he got to lose?

Gathering himself, he looks up from the menu: "How's about a quickie?"

Enraged by his insolence, the waitress flies off the handle, smacking the man in the face and screaming insults before storming off to see the manager. Having witnessed the entire event, a nearby diner leans across to the man and proffers some advice. "Don't mind me, but I think it's pronounced 'Quiche.'"

The fireman's code

Called out to a fire at a fashionable apartment block, a fireman arrives to find flames pouring out of an upstairs window, and a woman screaming. Donning protective gear, he climbs the ladder, enters the flat… and spies a curvy brunette in a see-through nightie.

"Amazing," says the fireman, "you're the third pregnant girl I've rescued this week."

"Hey," shouts the girl, indignantly, "I'm not pregnant."

"Yeah," the fireman smiles, "but you're not rescued yet either."

> # How do you make...
> ## ...five pounds of fat look good?
> *Put a nipple on it.*

Nuisance call

It's two o'clock in the morning and a husband and wife are asleep, when suddenly the phone rings. The husband picks up the phone and says, "Hello…? How the hell do I know? What am I, the weather man?" and promptly slams the phone down.

His wife rolls over and asks, "Who was that?"

The husband replies, "I don't know. Some bloke who wanted to know if the coast was clear."

The sex fence

A young boy went into a chemist's and asked for his first packet of johnnies. He was understandably nervous. The chemist, who was a woman in her sixties, asked, "What size?"

The boy didn't know. So the woman asked him to go out the back and size up. Round the back of the chemist's was a fence with three different-sized holes in it. As the boy put his knob in the first hole, the old woman surreptitiously ran round to the other side of the fence and started to suck away. The boy jumped back in amazement, then put his old fella in the second hole. Once again, the woman started to go at it like a sex-crazed dog. Again the boy jumped back.

He then put it in the third hole, and this time the woman bent over so he could poke her.

At this point he ran back to the front of the shop, where the old slag was waiting, panting. "W-w-well," she said, "what size were you?"

The boy replied, "To hell with the johnnies – how much do you want for that fence?"

Jacko dilemma

Michael Jackson's wife gives birth to a beautiful baby boy, but Jacko's a little concerned. "I just have to ask, doc," he says, taking his exhausted wife by the hand, "how long before we can have sex?"

"Well, Mike," says the doc, "I think you'd better leave it until he's at least walking…"

The blonde speeder

A traffic cop pulls alongside a speeding car on the motorway. Glancing at the car, he's astounded to see that the blonde behind the wheel is knitting. Not only that, the woman is obviously oblivious to his flashing lights and siren – and so he cranks down his window and turns on his loudhailer. "Pull over!" he shouts at the top of his voice.

"Nah," the blonde yells back, "it's going to be a scarf!"

> # What is an Essex girl's...
> ## ...idea of safe sex?
> *Putting the handbrake on.*

Q: WHAT IS THE DEFINITION OF A TAMPON?

Legless boozer

An Irishman's been drinking at a pub all night. When he stands up to leave he falls flat on his face. He tries to stand again, with the same result. So he figures he'll crawl outside and get some fresh air, and maybe that will sober him up. Once outside he stands up… and falls flat on his face.

So he decides to crawl down the four streets to his home. When he arrives at the door he stands up, and duly falls flat on his face again. He crawls through the door into his bedroom. When he reaches his bed, he tries one last time to get erect. This time he manages to pull himself upright, but he quickly falls right into bed and is sound asleep as soon as his head hits the pillow. He awakens the next morning to find his wife standing over him, shouting, "So you've been out drinking again!"

"What makes you say that?" says the Irishman, putting on an innocent look.

"The pub called," his wife says. "You left your wheelchair there again."

East country logic

A man was on holiday in Norfolk when he found he needed a new gas canister for his caravan, so he approached a local in the street and asked, "Excuse me, do you know if there's a B&Q in Norwich?"

"No," replied the bumpkin, "But there are two Es in Leeds."

Irish in space!

An Irishman and an American are arguing about who went into space first. The American is adamant that Uncle Sam was the first to put a man on the moon.

"What bollocks," replies the Irishman, "and anyhow, I hear that soon we'll be sending an Irish astronaut to the sun!" The American can't believe his ears. "Don't be so ridiculous," he laughs, "the fool would burn to death!"

"You great eejit," replies the Irishman. "We're not all stupid bastards… we're going to send him up at night."

A: DRACULA'S TEABAG.

What's white...
...and wiggles slowly across a disco floor?
Come dancing.

Rough justice

A judge is passing sentence on a prisoner and asks him, "Have you anything to say in your defence?"

To which the prisoner says, "Fuck all, Your Honour."

Shocked, the judge turns to the counsel for the defence and asks, "What did he say?"

"Fuck all, Your Honour," answers the barrister.

"That's funny," says the judge. "I could have sworn I saw his lips move."

The two experts

An off-duty doctor is walking by the side of a canal when he sees a man drowning in the murky waters. The man keeps going under, and is obviously taking in a lot of water. The doctor reaches out and manages to get a hold on the bloke and drags his upper body out of the canal, then turns him on his front, sits astride the body and starts pumping water out. There are gallons of shitty water spewing out of his mouth, plus tin cans, weeds, used condoms and loads of other crap. Suddenly, a second man turns up.

"You don't want to do that mate," he says.

"Listen," says the doc, "I'm a doctor. Don't try and tell me how to do my job."

"Well, I'm an engineer," says the second bloke. "And if you don't take that bloke's arse out of the canal you're going to pump it dry."

Special marking

A gay man visits a tattoo shop, has a good look at all the designs then finally plumps for a car to be tattooed onto his cock.

"Certainly, chum," says the tattooist, "what sort of car would you like?"

The man thinks for a moment. "Best make it a 4x4 – it's going to have to go through a lot of shit."

The pastor's wife

A large, burly man visits the local pastor's home and asks to see the minister's wife, a woman well known for her charitable impulses. "Madam," he says in a broken voice, "I wish to draw your attention to the terrible plight of a poor family in this parish. The father is dead, the mother is too ill to work and the nine children are starving. They are about to be turned into the cold, empty streets unless someone pays their rent, which amounts to £400."

"How terrible!" exclaims the preacher's wife. "May I ask who you are?"

The sympathetic visitor dabs his handkerchief to his eyes. "Yes," he sobs, "I'm the landlord."

Q: HOW DO YOU MAKE A BLONDE'S EYES TWINKLE?

Canine in trouble

Two friends are chatting. "My mum's got a new dog," says Dave.

"What's it called?" asks Bob.

"Minton," continues Dave. "He's a lovely dog, but he's got this weird habit of eating shuttlecocks."

"Shuttlecocks, eh," laughs Bob. "And he's called Minton? Weird. Have you tried to stop him eating them?"

"Oh yeah, but it's just no good," explains Dave. "I told him off last night. Pointed my finger at the bugger and shouted 'bad Minton!'"

The Lottery winner

A man runs home and kicks in the front door, yelling, "Pack your bags honey, I've just won the Lottery!"

"Oh, that's wonderful!" his wife says. "Should I pack for the beach or the mountains?"

"I don't care," he replies. "Just get the fuck out!"

New wife shocked

A young couple arrive at their hotel for the first night of their honeymoon – and immediately, they're frantically undressing each other. But when the husband removes his socks to reveal mangled, twisted toes, his wife has to stifle a scream.

"I had tolio as a child," he replies, by way of explanation.

"Don't you mean polio?" his bride asks.

"No, tolio. The disease only affected my toes."

Satisfied, his wife continues undressing – only to gasp again when she spies his lumpy and deformed legs.

"Oh," says her husband, seeing her alarm. "As a child, I also had kneasles."

"You mean measles?" she replies.

"No, kneasles – a very rare illness affecting the knees."

Smiling sympathetically, she continues undressing – until finally, her husband has stripped down to his underpants. Slowly, he pulls them down his legs – and his wife yelps again. "Let me guess," she says. "Smallcox?"

The randy parrot

A farmer and his wife are given a parrot by a relative. The male parrot soon sneaks out and screws the next door neighbour's turkeys. The neighbour knocks on the door and explains what the parrot has been doing. The owners of the parrot tell it if it doesn't stop they'll shave its head. But that night the parrot, overcome with

> # Did you hear about...
> ## ... the dyslexic pimp?
> *He bought a warehouse.*

desire, sneaks out and screws the neighbour's turkeys once again. So the next morning the man ties the bird down and shaves its head.

The following day is the farmer's daughter's wedding, and to please the relative who gave them the parrot they sit the randy bird on a piano. As a further punishment, they tell it that it has to greet all the guests and tell them where to sit in the church.

For an hour, the parrot does just fine. "Groom's side to the left, bride's side to the right," it squawks, until two bald guys walk in, when it screeches, "You two turkey-fuckers up on the piano with me!"

SHINE A TORCH IN HER EAR.

What does a tornado...
...have in common with a white trash divorce? Someone's always losing a trailer.

Perverted by language

Two men are driving down the road when a police car pulls them over. "Do you know you were doing 50 in a 30 area?" says the copper. "Short back and sides please," says the driver, "with a little off the top."

The policeman's naturally a little puzzled by this, but soldiers on. "Can I see your licence, sir?"

To which the driver replies, "A number one blended in up the back and nothing off the top please."

The policeman is getting angry by this time, and tells the driver, "If you don't co-operate I'll have to take you down the station!"

"A shampoo, please," the driver responds.

The policeman is by now very angry, and asks the passenger what's wrong with his mate. The man in the passenger seat replies, "Sorry, officer. My mate only speaks hairdo."

Starter's orders

Two guys are in a bar. One says to the other, "How's your sex life, buddy?"

"Not so good," the second bloke says. "Every time me and the missus have sex, she loses interest half-way through. It's very frustrating."

The first pauses, then says, "Yeah, I know what you mean. I used to have the same problem, but I found a cure. I hid a starter pistol under the bed. When she started to run out of steam, I simply fired the starter pistol. It gave her such a fright that she got all excited. She couldn't get enough! I wish I'd done it years ago."

Stunned but desperate, the other guy vows to try it that night. The next day they are back in the bar again. The first guy says, "How did you get on with the starter pistol?"

His irate pal says, "Don't talk to me about starter pistols! Last night we were having a little 69. As usual, she lost interest half-way through, so I fired the starter pistol just like you said."

"So what happened?"

"She bit my cock, shat in my face, and a man came out of the closet with his hands up!"

New sport on TV

The Olympic committee has just announced that Origami is to be introduced in Athens, 2004. Unfortunately it will only be available on paper view.

Why did the...
...leprechaun wear two condoms? To be sure, to be sure.

DID YOU HEAR ABOUT THE GIRL WHO WENT FISHING WITH

The sandwich-haters

An Englishman, an Irishman and a Scotsman are working on a building site, and they always sit at the top of their crane to eat their lunches together. The Englishman opens his lunchbox and looks at his sandwiches. "Cheese and fucking pickle," he mutters. "If I get cheese and pickle again tomorrow I'm going to jump off this crane." Next, the Scotsman opens his lunchbox and unwraps his sandwiches. "Ham!" he raves. "If the wife gives me ham again tomorrow, I'm going to jump off this crane!" Finally, the Irishman opens up his lunchbox. He too looks at his sandwiches in disgust. "Fucking jam again," he cusses. "If I get jam again tomorrow, I'm going to jump off this crane." The following day the three men are again at the top of the crane for their lunch. The Englishman opens up his lunchbox and is met with cheese and pickle sandwiches. As promised, he jumps off the crane. Next the Scotsman opens up his lunchbox, and he's got ham again. He jumps off. Lastly, the Irishman peers inside the lunchbox at his sandwiches. Jam. Without hesitation, he plunges off.

The three are buried together a few days later, where their wives get to talking. "I honestly didn't realise he no longer liked cheese and pickle," says the Englishman's wife. "My husband has always liked ham sandwiches. I just can't understand it," says the Scotsman's wife. "I'm at my wits end," says the Irishman's wife. "My husband always made his own sandwiches."

What's the difference...

...between a bumpy road and a prostitute?

A bumpy road knackers your tyres...

Boozer gets frisky

A drunk walked into a bar, looked around and approached a young lady. Without so much as an introduction, he placed his hand up her skirt and began fondling her. The woman jumped up and began screaming her head off. "Oh Christ! I'm so sorry," said the man, clearly embarrassed, "I thought you were my wife – you look exactly like her." "Why you drunken, worthless, insufferable heap of shit," screamed the woman, utterly incensed, "keep away from me!" "My God," said the man, "you sound just like her, too…"

Nun happy to please

A priest is transferred to a small convent. After meeting the Mother Superior and being shown the buildings, he decides to take a stroll into town and have a look around. Before long, a woman approaches him and whispers, "Hello, Father – how about a blow job for £20?" The priest ignores her and continues about his business, but as he trundles along another three women make him the very same offer. Bewildered, he returns to the convent, where Mother Superior asks how he enjoyed his trip. "Oh fine," he replies, "but I just want to know one thing – what's a blow job?" Mother Superior draws nearer and whispers, "Twenty quid, same as in town…"

Private takes praise

Pete joins the army. At the end of the first day his commanding officer is outraged. "Son, I did not see you in camouflage lesson today, you sack of shit!" "Sir," shouts Pete, "thank you very much, sir!"

The outraged punter

A man walks into a garage and tells the salesman he's in the market for a new car. "But there are no prices showing," he frowns. "How much is the blue Escort, for instance?" "Hmm," says the salesman, scratching his head. "That'll cost you two 20ft-long triangular coins and a pink note with a fluffy kitten on it." "I'm not paying that!" cries the punter. "That's silly money."

Why can't Miss Piggy...

...count to 70?

Because every time she gets to 69 she gets a frog in her throat.

A Scotsman, an Englishman and an Irishman...

...are sentenced to spend 15 years in solitary confinement. The judge, feeling sorry for the men, decides to allow each to take with him whatever he wants.

The Scotsman says, "I'd like to take a woman with me." The victim of his own logic, the judge reluctantly agrees, and the Scotsman takes his wife and heads off to solitary.

The Englishman says, "I'd like to take a telephone with me." The judge agrees, and off goes the Englishman with his telephone.

The Irishman pulls out a hand-held calculator and furiously punches the buttons for a few minutes. He then announces, "I'd like to take 3,000 cartons of cigarettes with me." The judge agrees, and off goes the Irishman with his fags.

After 15 years they open the Scotsman's cell, and out he comes with his woman and 15 children. "That wasnae so bad," he says.

The Englishman emerges and announces he is now a multimillionaire, having set up a successful business by telephone.

The Irishman then emerges, trembling like a leaf. "Anybody got a light?" he asks.

Vegetable lover

A man is driving home late one night, feeling very randy. As he passes a pumpkin patch, his mind starts to wander. He thinks to himself, pumpkins are soft and squishy inside... There's no-one around for miles, so he pulls over to the side of the road, picks out a nice juicy-looking pumpkin, cuts the appropriate size hole in it and begins to pump away. After a while he really starts getting into it, which means he doesn't notice a police car pulling up. The cop walks over and says, "Excuse me, sir, but do you realise that you are screwing a pumpkin?"

The man looks at the cop in complete horror, thinks fast and says, "A pumpkin? Shit – is it midnight already?"

A little too literal

Being massively overweight, a blonde asks her doctor for a suitable diet. "Okay," he says, "I'd recommend you eat regularly for two days, then skip a day. Repeat this procedure for two weeks and the next time I see you, you'll have lost at least five pounds."

Happy, the blonde goes away – only to return a fortnight later having lost at least 30 pounds. "That's amazing!" cries the doctor. "So you followed my instructions?" The blonde nods. "I'll tell you, though, I thought I was going to drop dead that third day."

"From hunger, you mean?" asks the doctor.

"No," she says. "From skipping."

A: A COMPUTER THAT NEVER GOES DOWN ON YOU.

How do you get...
...a one-handed Irishman out of a tree? *Wave to him.*

The virgins' wedding night

Two virgins are due to be married in three weeks' time. However, the man has a serious problem: he can never get an erection. So he goes to see his doctor and tells him the problem.

"I'll give you some pills," says the sympathetic medic. "If you don't get any results, come back to me."

A week later and no wood, so the man returns to the doctor. "Try these instead," says the quack. "They're extra-strength. If nothing happens, come back and see me again."

On the morning of the wedding, the bloke is back in the surgery. "Doctor, you've got to help me – nothing's happened." So the doctor takes a splint, ties the man's dick in it and wraps some clingfilm round the whole apparatus. Satisfied, the man goes off to get married. When the couple are alone in their honeymoon suite, the wife says, "I'll just go and put on something more comfy." When she re-emerges, she's wearing nothing but black leather boots and satin gloves. "See these tits?" she whispers. "Never been touched by any human being. See this pussy? Never had anyone near it."

Not wanting to be outdone, the man points to his dick in the splint and clingfilm and says, "How about this! Still in its wrapping!"

Two women bet

A blonde and a brunette are watching the 10 o'clock news. The lead story is about a man standing on top of a building, about to jump off. The brunette says to the blonde, "I bet you a tenner that man jumps."

The blonde says, "You're on!" Sure enough, the guy jumps off the building. So the blonde turns to the brunette and says, "Well I guess that's £10 I owe you."

The brunette turns to her, laughing. "It's okay – I actually saw the six o'clock news and I knew that he jumped."

"I saw the six o'clock news as well," says the blonde, "but I didn't think he'd do it twice."

The truth about sex changes

A man is sitting in the bar when a good-looking woman sits down next to him. "Hi, Bob," she says.

"Do I know you?" Bob replies.

"You sure do, Bob, it's Frank, your best friend."

"My God, Frank – is that really you?"

"Sure is. I went to Sweden and got a sex change!"

"Wow, that's amazing – the make-up and new hair sure had me fooled! Tell me something, does it hurt when they cut your penis off?"

"Yeah," says Frank, "that hurts. But not nearly as much as when they stick that metal tube into your head and suck half your brains out."

Q: *"DOCTOR, DOCTOR, MY HAIR KEEPS FALLING OUT. WHAT CAN*

The hillbilly wedding

A hillbilly gets married, and on his wedding night his new bride explains that she's a virgin, at which point the groom runs screaming from the bedroom back home to his father. When his dad asks what went wrong, the man repeats what his new bride told him. "You're quite right to come home, son," says the old man. If she ain't good enough for her own family, she sure ain't good enough for ours."

Reincarnated

A woman goes to a seance. "Is there anybody there?" asks the medium.
"Yes," a small voice replies.
"Is that you, Bert?" asks the woman.
"Yes," he replies.
"Are you all right?"
"Lovely," the voice replies.
"What's it like where you are?" asks the wife.
"It's great," he replies, "today I went swimming and did a bit of fishing."
"Oh," said his widow, "you never did any of that while you were alive."
"No," the voice says, "well, I'm a duck now."

YOU GIVE ME TO KEEP IT IN?" A: "A SHOEBOX. NEXT."

Front bottom dentistry

A little girl and a little boy are playing in the garden. All of a sudden the little boy drags the girl into the shed and says, "If you show me yours I'll show you mine." So the little girl takes off her little flowery dress and slides down her little knickers. At that moment the boy's mother comes into the shed and discovers them. Furious at what her son is doing, she sends the girl home crying and banishes the boy to his room to think about what he's done. "Don't come down till you can behave," she tells him.

A few hours later the boy comes down to see his mother, who by this time has realised that she must talk to her son about the incident. "You must never, ever touch girls down there again," she tells him. The little boy is confused by this and asks why, so his mother says, "Well, they have teeth down there and they'll bite you!" Terrified, the boy runs up to his room to count his fingers.

Soon the little boy becomes a big boy, getting the odd snog here and there but never anything more, as he's terrified of those teeth. It gets to his wedding night, and there he is in bed with his new wife, who by now is thinking she's never going to get a shag. Sure enough, her husband just kisses her and turns over to go to sleep. "Is that it then?" she asks. "What about the rest of it?" "I can't," the man says, "I'm too scared."

Thinking this sweet, his wife says, "Look – you have nothing to worry about. I'll show you what to do." But he's still scared, so she asks him why. Upon hearing about the teeth story she can hardly stop herself laughing, but to reassure her new husband she says, "I'll prove it to you: women do not have teeth in their fannies. Here – have a look." And she parts her legs so he can see. He gasps, and says, "With gums like that I'm not surprised."

Lawyer unsure

A man visits his lawyer to help settle his divorce proceedings. "But it says here she's divorcing you because you threw a trifle at her," says the solicitor.

"Yes," says the man, downcast. "Now she's claiming custardy."

> # Did you hear about the scarecrow...
> ## ...who won a Nobel prize?
> *He was out standing in his field.*

> # What's red and yellow...
> ## ...and looks good on hippies?
> *Fire.*

Q: WHAT'S BLACK, TRIANGULAR AND SINGS?

The celibacy test

Three young candidates for the priesthood have spent years at a seminary, until one day they're told by the monsignor that just one last hurdle lies between them and their vocation: the celibacy test. The monsignor leads them into a windowless room where he tells them to undress, then ties a small bell to each man's dick. Standing back, he claps his hands, and in waltzes a beautiful young woman wearing nothing but a belly-dancer costume. She begins to dance sensually around the first candidate. Ting-a-ling. "Oh Patrick," says the monsignor, "I'm so disappointed in your lack of control. Run along now and take a long, cold shower, and pray about your carnal weakness." The chastened candidate leaves. The woman proceeds to the second candidate, weaving seductively while peeling off layers of veils. As the last veil drops… ting-a-ling. "Giuseppe, Giuseppe," sighs the monsignor. "You too are unable to withstand your carnal desires. Off you go: take a long, cold shower and pray for forgiveness." The dancer continues dancing in front of the final candidate. Nothing. She writhes her by now naked body up and down against the young priestly candidate. No response. Finally, she quits. "Sergio, my son, I am truly proud of you," says the monsignor. "Only you have the true strength of character needed to become a priest. Now go and join your weaker brethren in the showers." Ting-a-ling.

A: KATE'S BUSH.

The four dogs

Four men were bragging about how smart their dogs were. The first man was an engineer, the second man an accountant, the third a chemist and the fourth worked for the local authorities. First, the engineer called to his dog, "T-Square, do your stuff!" T-square dutifully trotted over to a desk, took out some paper and a pen and promptly drew a circle, a square and a triangle. Everyone agreed that was pretty smart.

The careful monkey

A man walks into a pub with his pet monkey on his shoulder and orders a pint. While he's drinking, the monkey jumps onto the bar and starts cavorting. First it grabs some peanuts and eats them, then it grabs some sliced limes and stuffs them in his gob, and finally it jumps onto the pool table, grabs the cue ball, sticks it in his mouth and swallows it whole. Enraged, the barman screams at the man, "Did you see what your bloody monkey just did? He ate my cue ball!"

"That doesn't surprise me," replies the punter. "The little bastard eats everything in sight. I'll pay for the cue ball and other stuff." And he settles the bill and leaves.

Two weeks later he's back, once more with the monkey in tow. He orders a drink, and within minutes the monkey is running amok – until it finds a stray maraschino cherry on the bar. The monkey grabs the cherry, sticks it up his arse, pulls it out and eats it.

The bartender's disgusted. "Did you see what your monkey did now?" he shouts. "He stuck a cherry up his brown eye, then pulled it out and ate it!"

"That doesn't surprise me," replies the punter. "He still eats everything in sight, but ever since that damn cue ball he measures it first."

Q: WHY DO AUSTRALIANS WHISTLE WHEN THEY HAVE A SHIT?

> # Why do doctors...
> ## ...spank babies when they're born?
> *To knock the dicks off the dumb ones.*

Then the accountant called to his dog: "Slide Rule, do your stuff!" Slide Rule went out into the kitchen and returned with a dozen biscuits. He divided them into four equal piles of three biscuits each.

Everyone agreed that was good, but the chemist said his dog could do better. "Measure!" he barked. "Do your stuff!" So Measure got up, padded over to the fridge, took out a pint of milk, got a 10-ounce glass from the cupboard and poured exactly eight ounces in without spilling a drop. The local authority worker got to his feet. "Coffee Break," he said, "do your stuff!" So Coffee Break jumped to his feet, ate the cookies, drank the milk, dumped on the paper, sexually assaulted the other three dogs, claimed he'd injured his back while doing so, filed a grievance report for unsafe working conditions, put in for Worker's Compensation and went home on sick leave.

The smart poacher
Late one evening, a man is leaving a lake with two buckets of fish when he's stopped by a gamekeeper. "Excuse me, sir," says the keeper, "but I presume you have a licence to catch those fish?" The man smiles. "No, I haven't. But these are my pet fish." "Pet fish?" the gamekeeper replies incredulously.

"Yes, sir. Every night I take them to the lake and let them swim around for a while. When I whistle, they jump back into their buckets and I take them home." The gamekeeper frowns. "My arse!" he scoffs. "This I've got to see." "Okay," says the man, raising an eyebrow, and with that he turns back to the lake and pours the fish into the murky depths. For several minutes the pair watch the surface until the gamekeeper gets annoyed. "Well?" he cries, "when are you going to call them back?" "Call who back?" the man asks innocently. "The fish, of course." "Fish?" says the man, "what fish?"

> # Did you hear about...
> ## ...the new blonde paint?
> *It's cheap and it spreads easily.*

Did you hear about...
...the guy with five dicks?
His pants fit him like a glove.

Outsmarted

Hoping for an easy bust, a traffic copper stations himself outside a popular local pub and waits. As everyone floods out at closing time, he spots his quarry – a man so obviously bombed that he can barely walk. He stumbles around the car park for a few minutes, looking for his car. After trying his keys in five others, he finally finds his own vehicle – whereupon he sits for ten minutes as the other patrons leave, blinking slowly. Slowly, he turns his lights on, then off, wipers on then off, then starts to pull forward into the grass. Finally, alone in the car park, he pulls out onto the road and drives away.

Instantly, the policeman turns on the blue lights, pulls over the man and makes him blow into a breathalyser. However, the readout is 0.00.

"I don't understand," babbles the officer. "The equipment must be faulty."

"I doubt it," grins the man. "Tonight, I'm the Designated Decoy."

The musical octopus

A bloke walks into a bar, sits down and says to the bartender, "Pint of beer, please, and a glass of water for the octopus."

The bartender looks over and sure enough he has an octopus with him. "No animals allowed in here," he says. "And that includes octopuses."

"This is a special octopus," says the punter. "It can play any musical instrument."

"Right," says the bartender. "If your octopus can go over there and play that piano, I'll give you both the beer and the water for free."

So the octopus wanders over and plays the piano perfectly. Another customer comes over with a flute and says, "I bet you a tenner that your octopus can't play this flute." So the octopus picks it up and plays it perfectly, and the man hands over the money. Next a Scotsman walks over with some bagpipes and dares the octopus to play them. The animal seems puzzled, and simply looks at the instrument. "Go on!" shouts the man. "Play the bloody things!"

"Look, mate," says the octopus. "As soon as I can work out how to take its pyjamas off, I'm taking it home and fucking it."

Cross-dressing car

A motorist goes to his mechanic and says, "I think my car may be a transvestite."

"Are you having me on?" says the grease-monkey.

"No, straight up," says the motorist. "It keeps slipping into the wrong gear."

Why does an elephant...
...have four feet?
Because six inches isn't long enough.

Medical breakthrough

After a game of tennis Sam's arm was hurting, so he set off for the doctor's. "Don't do that," said his mate. "You'll have to spend an hour in the waiting room breathing in other people's germs. There's a computer at the chemist that can diagnose anything quicker and cheaper than a GP – just feed it a sample of your urine, and the computer will diagnose your problem and tell you what to do about it. And it only costs a tenner."

So Sam pissed in a jar, trooped down to the chemist's and paid the £10. The computer went back to the chemist's, poured in the sample and deposited a tenner.

The machine again made the usual noise and printed out the following analysis, "YOUR TAP WATER IS TOO HARD – GET A WATER SOFTENER. YOUR DOG HAS WORMS – GIVE HIM WORM PILLS. YOUR DAUGHTER IS USING COCAINE – PUT HER IN REHAB. YOUR WIFE IS PREGNANT WITH TWINS; THEY ARE NOT YOURS – GET A LAWYER. AND IF YOU DON'T STOP JERKING OFF, YOUR ELBOW WILL NEVER GET BETTER."

Teenie thug corrected

It's the day after Bonfire Night and little Tommy arrives at school looking miserable. The teacher calms the class down and says, "Tommy, I hear you were in a bit of trouble last night, weren't you?"
"Yes, miss," replies Tommy. "I was caught putting bangers up cats' arses."
The teacher corrects the young lad, "Rectum Tommy, rectum."
"Rectum, miss? I blew their bloody heads off!"

blooped, lights flashed, and after a brief pause out popped a small slip of paper. "YOU HAVE TENNIS ELBOW," it said. "SOAK YOUR ARM IN WARM SALT WATER. AVOID HEAVY LABOUR. IT WILL BE BETTER IN TWO WEEKS."

Later that evening, thinking how amazing this new technology was and how it would change medical science forever, Sam wondered if the machine could be fooled. So he mixed together some tap water, a stool sample from his dog and urine samples from his wife and daughter. To top it off, he cracked one off into the concoction. Then he

Talking clock

A drunk is proudly showing off his new flat to a couple of friends late one night, and leads the way to his bedroom, where there's a huge brass gong.

"What's that for?" asks one of the guests.

"That's the talking clock," replies the man. "Listen…" With that, he gives it a big whack with a hammer.

"For pity's sake!" screams a voice from next door, "it's ten past three in the morning!"

How do you call...

...all the squirrels in the world? *"Calling all squirrels, calling all squirrels..."*

The Scotch challenge

George Michael walks into a bar and says to the bartender, "I want you to give me 12-year-old Scotch, and don't try to fool me because I can tell the difference." The bartender is sceptical and decides to try to trick George with a glass of five-year-old. The leather-clad crooner takes a sip, scowls and says, "Bartender, this crap is five-year-old Scotch. I told you I want 12-year-old."

The bartender tries once more with eight-year-old Scotch. George takes a sip, grimaces and says, "Bartender, I don't want this eight-year-old filth. Give me 12-year-old Scotch!" Admitting defeat, the bartender dusts off the 12-year-old Scotch from the back of the bar. George takes a sip and sighs, "Ah... now that's the real thing." A disgusting, grimy, stinking drunk has been watching all this with great interest. He stumbles over and sets a glass down in front of George and says, "Pal – I'm impressed by what you can do. Try this one on me." George Michael takes a sip... and immediately spits out the liquid, crying, "Yechhh! This stuff tastes like piss!"

The drunk's eyes light up. "Aye!" he says. "Now how old am I?"

Statues come to life

There were two statues in the park – one of a boy and one of a girl. One day an angel fluttered by and clicked its fingers. The statues came to life. "I am the angel of the statues," said the heavenly vision. "I can bring you to life for only 15 minutes, but you're free to do anything you would do if you were human." The statues looked at each other. "There's something we've been wanting to do for ages. Can we really do *anything*?" "Yes, anything. But you only have 15 minutes." Not wanting to waste any more time, the boy grabbed the girl by the hand, they both jumped into a nearby bush, and there was a lot of giggling, thrashing and happy squealing. Finally they emerged, sweaty but very happy, and climbed onto their pedestals. The angel clicked its fingers and they both turned back into stone. They looked no different, except they had smirks on their faces. The angel flew

Did you hear about...

...the dumb terrorist who tried to blow up a bus? *He burnt his lips on the exhaust.*

WHAT DO YOU CALL A WELSHMAN WITH A SHEEP UNDER

The fussy whale

A male whale and a female whale are swimming off the coast of Japan when they notice a whaling ship. The male whale recognises it as the same ship that had harpooned his father many years earlier. Thirsting for revenge, he says to the female whale, "Let's both swim under the ship and blow out of our air-holes at the same time. It should cause the thing to turn over and sink."
They try it and, sure enough, the ship turns over and quickly sinks. Soon, however, the whales realise that the sailors have jumped overboard and are swimming to the safety of the shore. The male is enraged by the possibility of blubber-lovers getting away and tells the female, "Let's swim after the bastards and gobble them up before they reach the shore."
Racing after the struggling swabbies, he realises the female is reluctant to follow him.
"Look," she explains, "I went along with the blow job, but I absolutely refuse to swallow the seamen."

off into the distance. A few minutes later, the angel returned and clicked its fingers again. The statues looked a bit surprised, and the angel said, "I'm not really allowed to do this, but you looked so happy, I thought I'd come back and give you another 15 minutes of life. Remember, you can do whatever you want."
"Excellent! Let's do it again!" said the boy statue.
"Why don't we do it the other way round, this time?" replied the girl statue. "You hold the pigeon down and I'll crap on its head."

Pre-natal dilemma

A woman is six months pregnant with her first child, and is visiting her obstetrician for a check-up. Just as the examination is finishing, she turns to the doctor, "Um, this is sort of awkward… my husband wants me to ask you…"

"Really, don't worry, I get this question all the time," says the doctor, placing a reassuring hand on her shoulder. "Sex is absolutely fine until late in the pregnancy."

"Er… no," continues the woman. "He wants to know if I can still mow the lawn."

Girl kind to pet

A little girl walks into a pet shop and approaches the counter. "Excuthe me, mithter," she asks in the sweetest little lisp, "do you keep wittle wabbith?" Smiling, the shopkeeper gets down on his knees, so that he's on her level. "Well," he asks, "do you want a wittle white wabby? Or a soft and fuwwy black wabby? Or one like that cute wittle brown wabby over there?"

The little girl leans forward herself. "Hmm," she says in a quiet voice, "I don't fink my pyfon weally giveth a toth."

The flavoured johnnies

A chap is in the pub with his wife. After the man goes for a slash, he comes back bursting with excitement. "You'll never guess what they've got in there!" he tells his missus. "Condoms – fancy ones! They've got all different flavours – banana, strawberry, chocolate! They've even got piña colada and whisky flavours!"

"Nip back in and get a packet," says the wife, "and we'll try them out later."

Back home later that night, the couple retire to bed with their new toys. "Let's play a game," says the husband. "I'll turn out the lights, put on a condom and you have to guess the flavour."

"Okay," says his wife, and the lights go out. "Cheese and onion!" she exclaims 30 seconds later.

"Wait till I get it on first!" says hubbie.

Sticky seat

A man was decorating his bathroom, and had just applied the last coat of varnish to the toilet seat. He left the room for a minute to get a mug of cocoa, but when he came back he found his wife stuck to the seat. So he unscrewed the seat and took his wife – still attached – to the hospital.

After an hour the couple finally got to see the doctor. "What seems to be the problem?" asked the medic, and the man turned his wife around and lifted her skirt up. After several minutes of the doctor looking at and feeling his wife's arse, the worried man said, "So?"

The doc straightened up.

Did you hear about the crab… …who went to the disco? *He pulled a muscle.*

What do you give a man...
...who's got everything? *Penicillin.*

"It's beautiful," he said, "but why did you get it framed?"

The three sisters' hot dates

Three sisters are sat in their bedroom discussing what they're going to do that night. While deciding, they hear a knock at the front door. Their dad answers it, to find a lad standing there. "Hiya," says the youth. "My name's Lance – I've come to pick up Flance to take her to the dance. Any chance?" "Sure," says the dad, and with this Flance leaves for the dance with Lance. A short while later there's another knock at the door. Again the dad answers. It's another lad. "Hello, sir," he says, "I'm Joe, I've come to pick up Flo to take her to the show. Can she go?" The dad nods his okay, and away goes Flo to the show. The one girl left on her own feels a bit left out, when finally there's another knock at the door. Again the dad answers. "Wotcher," says the young man on the doorstep. "My name's Tucker..." "You can piss off!" shouts the dad as he slams the door shut.

New shoe range

Have you heard about "Dike", the new running shoe for lesbians? It has an extra long tongue and only takes one finger to get off.

Welcome to Australia

An English emigrant steps off the plane in Australia, clutching his citizenship papers and eagerly awaiting his first meeting with a genuine Aussie. But no sooner has he left the airport than he's appalled to see a young man humping a kangaroo. Shocked but undeterred, he continues his journey – but is again flabbergasted to see another man banging away at yet another kangaroo. He's stunned and sickened, so heads for the nearest bar. There on the steps is a crusty, old, one-legged Australian, jerking himself off. "What the hell is wrong with you people?" shouts the immigrant. "I've just seen two men shagging kangaroos, and now I find you rubbing off outside the local boozer!" "Come on, mate," says the oldster. "You don't expect me to catch a kangaroo with only one leg, do you?"

What do you call...
...a Teletubbie that's been burgled? *Tubbie.*

Irishman abroad

An Irishman had been in Germany looking for work, and on returning to the old country his drinking buddies pressed him for stories about his trip into the big, wide world.

"I stepped off the boat in Hamburg," said the Irishman, "and there was this big redhead waving to me as I walked ashore. 'Hey, Irish!' she shouted, 'how would you like to come with me for the time of your life?' I thought, lovely girl, why not? And yes, I had the time of my life! Next morning she brought me breakfast in bed, a bloody feast I had. But I was starting work that day, so I put on my coat and set off down the stairs. This girl called after me, 'Hey, Irish! How about some Marks?' So I gave her nine out of ten."

Romeo rejected

A pub regular starts to notice that, every evening, a very attractive woman comes in around 8pm and sits at the end of the bar, always alone. After two weeks of seeing her there, he makes his move. "No thank you," she rebuffs him politely. "You see, this may sound rather odd in this day and age, but I'm keeping myself pure until I meet the man I love."

"That must be rather difficult," replies the man. "Oh, I don't mind too much," she says, nodding,

> # Who invented football?
> **Jesus. *He went up for the cross but was nailed by two defenders.***

"but it seems to have upset my husband."

Sex life spiced up

A couple had been married for six years, and were having trouble with their sex life: all the husband wanted to do was watch the football on telly. So the wife went to the psychiatrist. He asked her if she had tried aphrodisiacs and she said, "Yes, I've tried everything." He then asked her if she'd tried crotchless knickers. She hadn't, so she went out and bought some. Back home, she put them on underneath a very short mini-skirt. As usual, the husband was sitting watching the football. She walked in and sat down opposite him, and folded her legs. He looked up and frowned. She then unfolded her legs very slowly and widely, a number

Late night caller

Late one evening, a man is watching television when his phone rings. "Hello?" he answers. "Is that 77777?" sounds a desperate voice on the other end of the phone.

"Er, yes, it is," replies the man, puzzled.

"Thank God!" cries the caller, relieved. "Can you ring 999 for me? I've got my finger stuck in the number seven."

Q: HOW DO YOU KNOW WHEN YOUR WIFE HAS DIED?

Drunk drivers

Bill and Dave are walking home after a night on the sauce. They've no money and are staggering all over the place when they find themselves outside a bus depot. Bill has a brainwave, "Go and steal us a bus so we can drive home – I'll stay on the lookout."

Dave agrees and breaks into the garage. He's gone nearly 20 minutes before Bill catches sight of him again.

"What the hell are you doing, Dave?" he shouts. "Get a move on!"

"But I can't find a number three anywhere…" says Dave.

"You idiot," shouts Bill, stunned by his friend's stupidity, "steal a number 11! We'll get off at the Arndale and walk the rest of the way!"

of times. The husband didn't flinch.

So she thought, "Bugger it," and spread them. The husband looked over in horror and said, "Are those crotchless knickers you're wearing?"

"Yes," she purred. "Why?"

"Thank Christ for that," said the husband. "I thought it was a rip in the new sofa."

Spuds you misunderstand

A man strolls into his local grocer's and says, "Three pounds of potatoes, please."

"No, no, no," replies the owner, shaking his head, "it's kilos nowadays, mate…"

"Oh," apologises the man, "three pounds of kilos, please."

The parrot's pedigree

A woman goes into a pet shop intending to buy a parrot, not realising how expensive the things are. Once inside the shop she begins looking around and discovers that she can't afford any of the multicoloured birds on offer, so she goes up to the owner and asks him if he has anything cheaper. He takes her out back and shows her the dirtiest, ugliest-looking parrot she has ever seen, explaining that it was donated by the local brothel. Desperate for some feathered companionship, she buys it and takes it home. Later that day her daughter pays her a visit. The parrot, which had been silent to that point, suddenly pipes up, "New whore house! New whore!"

Embarrassed, the mother explains to her daughter why the parrot said this. An hour later the woman's next door neighbour drops in for a cuppa, and once again the parrot jumps into life. "New whore house!" the evil creature squawks. "New whore!" Once again, the woman is left to make her awkward explanation. Later that night the woman's husband comes home from work. The parrot looks at him for a minute, then screeches, "How's it going, John?"

Miracle birth

A woman is dating a surgeon and, before long, she becomes pregnant. She doesn't want an abortion, so the doc says he'll come up with a plan. Nine months later, just as the woman is due to give birth, a priest goes into the hospital for a prostate gland infection. The doctor says to the woman, "I know what we'll do. After I've operated on the priest, I'll give the baby to him and tell him it was a miracle." So the surgeon delivers the baby then operates on the priest. After the op he goes in to the man of God and tells him, "Father, you're not going to believe this."

"What?" asks the priest, "what happened?"

"You gave birth to a child!"

"But that's impossible!" says the priest.

"I did the operation myself," insists the doctor, "it's a miracle. Here's your baby." Fifteen years go by, and the priest realises it's time to tell his son the truth. So he sits the boy down and says, "Son, I have something to tell you. I'm not your father."

Q: WHY ARE WOMEN LIKE CONDOMS? A: THEY SPEND 90 PER CENT OF

> # What do you have...
> ## ...if you've got a green ball in one hand and a green ball in the other?
> *Complete control of Kermit the frog.*

The son says, "What do you mean, you're not my father?" "I'm actually your mother," the priest replies. "The archbishop is your father."

Thirsty playwright

William Shakespeare walks into a pub and asks the barman for a pint of lager. "On your way, son," says the barman. "I'm not serving you."

Perplexed, Mr Shakespeare repeats his request, only to evoke a similar response. "Look, pal," says Shakespeare. "I've nothing against you or your pub – all I want is a pint of ale. Now be a good lad and get on with it, eh?"

The barman, getting shirty now, looks Will up and down and, with considerable anger in his voice, asks the famous gent to leave. Shakespeare looks forlorn. "Why?" he says. "What have I done?" The barman grips him by the collar and whispers in his ear, "You're Bard!"

Woman drops baby

A house catches fire, and there's a woman trapped on the top floor with her baby. She's leaning out the window screaming for help when the firefighters arrive. One of the firemen runs over and shouts to her, "Throw me your baby!"

"No!" screams the woman. "You'll drop him!"

The fireman insists. "It's okay," he tells her. "I was a Premiership goalkeeper for ten years. I'll catch him." So the woman relents, tossing her baby down. And the fireman catches it, bounces it twice and kicks it over a wall.

Lord seeks graft

Looking for work, Jesus goes to the local Job Centre. "Okay, Mr Christ," says the assistant, after typing in his details, "there are two jobs that come up for your spec. One is a carpenter in Jerusalem at £2,000 per week; the other a carpenter in Aberdeen at £200 a week."

And lo, the Son of God did speak, "I'll take the one in Aberdeen, cheers."

The assistant is surprised. "Why? You'd get far more money in the other job."

"I know," Jesus spake thus. "But the last time I worked in Jerusalem I got hammered with tax."

THEIR TIME IN YOUR WALLET AND THE OTHER 10 PER CENT ON YOUR DICK.

What do you call...
...a condom strolling down the street? *Johnny Walker.*

The English copper

An English policeman starts his first day of work in Ireland. Being new on the job he wants to look good in front of his fellow workers. While he is sitting in a lay-by looking for speeders, he spots a Ferrari driving past. "Right," he thinks, "the perfect opportunity to impress my colleagues." So he sets off, sirens blazing, and stops the driver, intending to provoke the man so he can arrest him.

Irishman is still standing in the circle, looking completely calm. So the cop turns back around and smashes the windscreen. Once again he spins round – but the Irishman has a smirk on his face!

Not believing his eyes, the policeman smashes the windows. Once again he turns, to find the Irishman pissing himself. Now he gets out a penknife and slashes all four tyres. When he looks up, the Irishman is actually rolling around on the road in fits of hysterics.

"What's so funny, Paddy?" says the cop. "I just smashed up your new Ferrari!"

"I know," says the Irishman. "But what you didn't see was that when you turned around I stepped out of the circle!"

Fisherman gives wife ultimatum

Waking one sunny morning, a man turns to his wife and tells her they're going fishing for the day. "Oh no – I'm not

In the beginning...

God is talking to one of his angels. He says, "Boy, I just created a 24-hour period of alternating light and darkness on Earth."

"What are you going to do now?" asks the angel.

"Call it a day," says God.

"Could you step out of the car, sir." The Irishman behind the wheel obliges. "Right sir," says the cop, "I'm going to draw this circle of chalk on the ground. You must stay in it at all times." "All right, officer," says the Irishman.

Then, with the Irishman standing in the circle, the cop walks over to the car, gets out his truncheon and breaks the car's headlight. He then turns around, and to his surprise sees that the

wasting a lovely day like this," replies his wife. "Besides, you know how much I hate fishing."

"Okay," answers the man, "you have three choices: me, you and the dog go fishing; you give me a blow job; or you take it up the tradesman's. I'm off to the shed for ten minutes, and I want your decision when I get back."

A few minutes later he returns. "I've decided on the blow job," his wife says.

Q: WHY DID THE PERVERT CROSS THE ROAD?

It is easier for a camel...

A teacher, a dustman and a lawyer find themselves waiting outside the Pearly Gates. Eventually Saint Peter emerges and informs them that in order to get into Heaven, they'll each have to answer one question. Peter turns first to the teacher. "What was the name of the ship that crashed into the iceberg? They just made a movie about it."
The teacher answers quickly, "That would be the *Titanic*." Saint Peter lets him through the gate.
He then turns to the dustman and says: "How many people died on the ship?" Fortunately for him, the trash-collector had just seen the movie. "1,228," he answers.
"That's right! You may enter." Peter then turns to the lawyer. "Name them."

"Good," he says, losing no time in dropping his trousers.
But just as she kneels down to perform the act, the wife notices a strange smell. "But your crotch reeks of shit!" she cries.
"Yeah," says her husband, nonchalantly. "The dog didn't want to go fishing either."

Brooms to be

Two brooms are standing in a closet. Before long they're chatting away – within a week, they're married. On the big day the bride broom looks stunning in her white dress; the groom broom suave in his suit. The ceremony is wonderful, and soon everyone is seated at dinner. The bride broom leans across and whispers to her husband, "I've a surprise… I think we're going to have a little broom!"
"That's impossible," shouts the angry broom, "we haven't even swept together!"

Fragrance misplaced

Two blondes walk into the perfume section of a department store and pick up a sample bottle. The first blonde sprays it on her wrist and smells it.
"That's quite nice," she coos. "What's it called?"
"It says 'Viens à moi' on the label," replies her friend.
"Viens à moi?" says the first bonde, "what the hell does that mean?"
At this stage the assistant offers some help. "Viens à moi, ladies, is French for 'come to me'."
The first blonde takes another sniff, "Here, Kerry," she says offering her arm to her mate. "It doesn't smell like come to me. Does that smell like come to you?"

Moscow table manners...
What does a Russian use to wipe his mouth after dinner? *A Soviet.*

A: HE COULDN'T GET HIS KNOB OUT OF THE CHICKEN!

The decorating nuns

Two nuns are ordered to paint a room in the convent, and Mother Superior's last instruction is that they must not get one drop of paint on their new habits. After conferring about this, the two nuns decide to lock the door of the room, strip off and paint in the nude. In the middle of the project there comes a knock at the door. "Who is it?" calls one of the nuns.

"Blind man," replies a voice from the other side of the door.

The two nuns look at each other, shrug and, deciding that no harm can come from letting a blind man into the room, they open the door. "Nice tits," says the man. "Where do you want these blinds?"

Unauthorised withdrawal

A bloke in a balaclava bursts into a sperm bank, armed with a shotgun. "Open the safe!" he yells at the terrified girl at reception.

"But we're not a real bank," she stammers. "We don't have any money. This is a sperm bank."

"Don't argue – open the safe or I'll blow your head off!" screams the guy with the gun. The terrified woman obliges. Once she's opened the safe door, the guy says, "Take out one of the bottles and drink it!"

"But it's full of spunk!" the poor girl replies.

"Don't argue! Just drink it!" says the gunman. So she prises the cap off one of the bottles and gulps it down.

"Take another one out and drink that too!" demands the gunman. She does as she's told. Suddenly the man pulls off his balaclava and, to the receptionist's amazement, it's her husband.

"There," he says, "it's not that bloody difficult, is it?"

Q: HOW MANY TIMES DOES 59 GO INTO 21?

How do you spot...
...a blind man in a nudist camp?
It's not hard.

Disappointing opening

The first day at the London sperm bank was pretty unsuccessful. Only two blokes made appointments. One came on the bus and the other missed the tube.

Sheep love

A researcher is conducting a survey into sheep shagging. First of all he visits a Cornish farmer. "So, Cornish farmer, how do you shag your sheep?" he asks.

"Well, I take the hind legs of the sheep and put them down my wellies, and take the front legs of the sheep and put them over a wall," the yokel replies.

"That's very interesting," says the researcher, and he gets on a train to the Midlands. "So, Midlands farmer, how do you shag your sheep?" he asks.

"Well, I take the hind legs of the sheep and put them down my wellies and take the front legs of the sheep and put them over a wall," replies the old scrote.

"That's very interesting," says the researcher. "That's how they do it in Cornwall too." And he gets on a plane to Aberdeen.

"So, Aberdeenshire farmer, how do you shag your sheep?"

"Well, I take the hind legs of the sheep and put them down my wellies, and take the front legs of the sheep and put them over my shoulders."

"Over your shoulders?" quizzes the researcher. "Don't you put them over a wall like everyone else?"

"What?" says the Scottish farmer. "And miss out on all the kissing?"

Smart thinking

A married man was having an affair with his secretary. Not for the first time, their passions overcame them at work and they took off for her house, where they made passionate love all afternoon. Exhausted from the wild sex, they then fell asleep, awakening around eight in the evening. As the man threw on his clothes he told the woman to take his shoes outside and rub them through the grass and dirt. Mystified, she nonetheless complied.

He then slipped into his shoes and drove home.

"Where have you been?" demanded his wife when he entered the house.

"Darling, I can't lie to you," said the man. "I've been having an affair with my secretary and we've been screwing like rabbits all day." The wife glanced down at his shoes and said, "You lying bastard! You've been playing golf again!"

How do you make...
...a dog drink?
Put it in a liquidiser.

What's the name... ...of the active ingredient in Viagra? Mycoxafailin.

The stray earring

A mechanic is at work one day when he notices that his fellow grease-monkey is wearing an earring. This man knows his co-worker to be a conservative fellow, and is curious about this sudden change in fashion sense. "Tom, I didn't know you were into earrings," he says. "Oh, sure," replies Tom sheepishly. "Really? How long have you been wearing one?" asks the mechanic. "Ever since my wife found it in our bed."

At the playschool

As a class project, a playschool teacher asks her pupils what, out of all the materials in the world, they would like to be made of. Quickly, one little boy's arm shoots up. "I would be made out of gold, miss," he squeaks. "Then I could scratch my arm and use a few flakes of gold to buy a new car."

Another young cherub pipes up. "Miss, miss!" he cries. "I'd be made of platinum. It's worth more than gold, and a few flakes could buy two cars."

"And what about you, Johnny?" asks the teacher of the little boy at the back. "Simple, miss," replies Johnny. "Pubic hair."

"Why on Earth would you want to be made out of that?" asks the teacher, aghast.

"Well, my older sister's only got a little," the youngster replies. "But you should see the number of cars outside our house."

The escaped gorillas

Three gorillas escape from the zoo, and the director decides to hire a professional hunter to recapture them. The hunter accepts and goes to assess the situation. "I should be able to get them back for you," he says, "All I need is a dozen helpers with nets, a couple of vans, my dog and my shotgun." Having acquired the equipment, the hunter and the zoo director head off into a nearby forest, where they quickly locate the gorillas up three separate trees. The hunter makes his way up to the first tree and gives it a good shake. The unfortunate gorilla falls to

Nice bird

A man is talking to a woman at the bar, when he looks at her and asks, "Have you ever had a magpie on your left wrist?"

"No," the lady replies.

"Okay. Have you ever had a parrot on your right wrist?" the man continues.

"No," the lady replies.

The man then gets the woman to poke out her tongue. "Well," he says, "it looks like you've had a cockatoo on there."

Q: WHAT'S THE DEFINITION OF AN ITALIAN VIRGIN?

The bottle opener

One day, after striking gold in Alaska, a lonesome miner came down from the mountains and walked into a saloon in the nearest town. "I'm lookin' fer the meanest, roughest, toughest whore in the Yukon!" he growled to the bartender. "Well, we got her!" barked the barkeep. "She's upstairs – second room on the right." The miner handed the bartender a gold nugget to pay for the whore and two beers. He grabbed the bottles, stomped up the stairs, kicked open the second door on the right and yelled, "I'm lookin' for the meanest, roughest, toughest whore in the Yukon!"

The woman inside the room looked at the miner and said, "Well, you found her!" She then stripped naked, bent over and grabbed both ankles. "How'd ya know I like to do it in that position?" asked the miner.

"I didn't," replied the whore, "but I thought ya might like to open them beers before we get started."

the floor, where the hunter's dog toddles up to it and bites off his knackers before the helpers drag him off into the van.

The same thing happens to the second gorilla.

The third is reluctant to come down, however, so the hunter decides to climb up the tree and coax it down with a banana. The zoo director calls up to him, "If it attacks you, shall I shoot it with the shotgun?"

"No!" the hunter shouts down, "but if I fall out of this tree, shoot the fucking dog!"

A: A GIRL WHO CAN RUN FASTER THAN HER BROTHER.

Why do sumo wrestlers... ...shave their legs? *To avoid being mistaken for feminists.*

Atishoo!

A man and a woman are riding next to each other in first class. The man sneezes, pulls out his wang and wipes the tip off. The woman can't believe what she just saw and decides she is hallucinating. A few minutes pass. The man sneezes again. He pulls out his wang and wipes the tip off. The woman is seething – she can't believe such an uncouth person exists. A few minutes pass. The man sneezes yet again. He takes his wang out and wipes the tip off. The woman has finally had enough. She turns to the man and says, "Three times you've sneezed, and three times you've removed your penis from your pants to wipe it off! What the hell kind of degenerate are you?"

"I'm so sorry to have disturbed you, ma'am," the man apologises. "The fact is that I have a very rare condition. When I sneeze, I have an orgasm."

The woman looks aghast. "I'm so sorry! What are you taking for it?"

"Pepper."

The naked rescuer

A young couple go out for a drive one evening. While bombing down the road the man says to the girl, "If I go at 100 miles an hour, will you take off your clothes?" She agrees and he begins to speed up. When the speedometer hits a ton she starts to strip. When she gets all her clothes off he is so busy staring at her that he drives off the road and flips the car.

The girl is thrown clear without a scratch, but her clothes and her boyfriend are trapped in the car. "Go get help!" he pleads.

"I can't," she replies, "I'm naked."

He points to his shoe that was thrown from the car and says, "Cover your snatch with that and go get help." So she takes his shoe, covers herself up and runs to the petrol station down the road. When she arrives she's frantic, and yells to the attendant, "Help me! My boyfriend's stuck!"

The attendant looks down at the shoe covering her crotch and replies, "I'm sorry, miss. He's too far in."

What's orange... ...and sounds like a parrot? *A carrot.*

Battle of the sexes

If your wife comes out of the kitchen to shout at you, what have you usually done wrong?
Made her chain too long.

Last request denied

Jim returns from the doctor's and tells his wife he only has 24 hours to live. After an emotional last dinner together, he asks her for his final request: to make love to him. Of course, she agrees – and half an hour later, they collapse in each other's arms. A few hours later, however, Jim gets restless. "Honey," he calls, waking his wife, "could we perhaps make love again?" Nodding sadly, his wife agrees – and after some athletic love-making, she falls asleep once more. But a few hours on, Jim still isn't satisfied and wakes her again. "Honey?" he moans. "Just one more time, before I die in… six hours?" Exhausted, she nevertheless agrees – then rolls over and falls asleep. Finally, Jim can't bear it any longer and taps her on the shoulder once again. But before he can speak, she sits up abruptly. "Listen, Jim," she snarls. "I have to get up early in the morning. You don't."

Pilot entertains Geordies

An aeroplane returning from a hot Spanish resort is coming in to land at Newcastle Airport. The captain gets onto the PA, "On behalf of this airline I'd like to thank you for flying with us. The temperature outside is 19 degrees and it's a beautiful day. I hope you enjoyed your flight and I look forward to seeing you again soon. Thank you."

Unfortunately, the captain mistakenly leaves the tannoy switched on, which means that after the plane has landed everyone hears him exclaim to his co-pilot, "Right – I'm going for a shit, then I'm going to shag that new hostess."
The passengers are astonished, while from the rear of the plane comes the sound of crashing trays and plastic plates, followed by a furious air hostess storming towards the front of the plane.
Just as she comes up to First Class, a man sticks his arm out to stop her. "You'll have to wait for that shag, pet," says the bloke. "He's gann' for a shit first."

The dead cat

An old maid wanted to travel by bus to the pet cemetery with the remains of her cat. As she boarded the bus, she whispered to the driver, "I have a dead pussy."
The driver pointed to the woman in the seat behind him. "Sit next to my wife," he said. "You two have a lot in common."

One-armed combat

Bruised and battered, Paddy hobbles into his local pub on a crutch with one arm in a cast. "My God!" the barman says. "What happened to you?
"I got in a tiff with Riley," groans Paddy.
"Riley? He's just a wee fellow," cries the surprised barkeep. "He must have had something in his hand."
"Aye, that he did," Kelly grimaces. "A shovel, it was."
"Dear Lord," nods the landlord. "Didn't you have anything in your hand?"
"Aye, I did – Mrs Riley's left tit," nods Paddy. "A beautiful thing it was, too. But not much use in a fight."

DOWN AN ELF'S PANTS: THEN SHE'S A GOBLIN.

Nudist colony #1

Who's the most popular woman in a nudist colony?
The one who can eat the last doughnut.

Constructive dismissal

A man walks into the dole office and asks to sign on. "What was your previous job?" asks the clerk. "I worked in a butcher's shop," replies the fella. "And why did you leave?" "I was sacked for putting my knob in the meat grinder," comes the reply. The clerk ponders this for a bit and says, "Oh, right… what happened, by the way?" "She got sacked as well."

Stone misread

Two tramps walk past a church and start to read the gravestones. The first tramp says, "Bloody hell – this bloke was 182!" "Oh yeah?" says the other. "What was his name?" "Miles, from London."

The wall-walker

A bloke strolls into a pub and walks up the wall, across the ceiling, back down the other wall then over to the bar, where he orders two whiskies. He drinks them, walks up the wall, across the ceiling, back down the other wall and out the door "That's strange," said a punter to the barman. "I know," the barman replies. "He normally orders a pint."

Blowing smoke

Three young kids are smoking behind the barn. "My dad can blow smoke through his nose," says the first boy. "That's nothing," says the second. "Mine can blow smoke through his ears." "You think that's good," says the third. "Mine can blow smoke through his arse. And I've seen the nicotine stains in his pants to prove it."

Heads it's "yes"…

Arriving for her university entrance exam, a blonde is overjoyed to find the questions all have Yes/No answers. Staring at the question paper for five minutes, she realises she still hasn't a clue. So, in a fit of inspiration, she takes a coin out of her purse and starts flipping it – marking a "Yes" for heads and "No" for tails. Within half an hour she's finished – but she still spends the last few minutes desperately throwing the coin, sweating and muttering. Alarmed, the examiner wanders over and asks what's wrong. "I want to be thorough," she cries. "So I'm rechecking my answers."

Did you hear about the monk…

…who got his dick caught in the bell-rope? *He told himself off.*

Plum in the mouth

Three young women are discussing their boyfriends over coffee.
"It's funny," says the first, "Pete's balls are always cold as ice when I'm sucking his cock…"
"Weird," replies the second girl, "it's the same with my Richard…"
They turn to their friend, "What about you? When you blow your man, are his balls cold?"
"Eugh, that's disgusting," spits the girl. "I never put his pee-pee in my mouth!"

"You're crazy," laugh her friends. "A good blow job is the best way to keep a man! Try it!"
The next morning they meet at the café, and the blow job novice is sporting a nasty shiner.
"Yep… the bastard hit me last night while I was sucking him off," she sniffs.
"What for?" ask her friends.
"I don't know," replies the girl. "All I did was tell him how strange it was that his balls were so warm, seeing as Pete and Richard's are always so cold…"

Honeymoon etiquette

A nervous young bride became irritated by her husband's lusty advances on their wedding night, and reprimanded him severely.
"I demand proper manners in bed," she declared, "just as I do at the dinner table."
Amused by his wife's formality, the groom smoothed his rumpled hair and climbed quietly between the sheets. "Is that better?" he asked, with a hint of a smile.
"Yes," replied the girl, "much better."
"Very good, darling," the husband whispered. "Now would you be so kind as to pass your tits."

Nudist colony #2

Who is the most popular man in a nudist colony?
The bloke who can hold two cups of coffee and nine doughnuts.

A: HE THOUGHT THAT NOBODY IMPORTANT WAS OUT TO GET HIM.

Did you hear about the bloke...

...who tried to flush his Viagra down the loo? The toilet seat stayed up for a month.

The squirrel test

President Bush is worried about the efficiency of his law enforcement agencies, so he decides to test them. He fences off a large area of woodland into three equal areas, then releases a red squirrel into each. He assigns the first area to the FBI, the second to the CIA and the third to the NYPD, giving each the mission of finding the squirrel within a week. Seven days elapse and Dubya checks on the agencies. The FBI say that they mobilised the Department of the Environment, the local police and the Forestry Commission but the squirrel was still at large.

The CIA explain that they called in a "Grey Ops" specialist who asked for a napalm strike, and they present a clear plastic envelope containing a pile of greasy grey ashes, saying they believe these to be red squirrel residue. When it's the turn of the NYPD to show their results, two cops walk in holding a handcuffed, bruised and blooded badger between them. The cops jab their night-sticks into the badger's ribs and say, "Tell him what you told us."

"I'm a red squirrel!" screams the badger. "I'm a red squirrel!"

Love in Scotland

A young Scottish lad and lassie are holding hands and gazing out over the loch. After a few minutes, the girl says to the boy, "A penny for your thoughts, Angus."

"I was thinkin'... perhaps it's time we had a wee cuddle." Blushing, the girl leans over and cuddles him.

After a while, the girl says, "Another penny for your thoughts, Angus."

"I was thinkin'... perhaps it's aboot time for a wee kiss." She leans over and pecks him lightly on the cheek.

There's another silence before the girl pipes up, "Another penny for your thoughts, Angus."

"I was thinkin'... perhaps it's aboot time ah poot ma hand on your leg."

Shyly, she puts his hand on her knee. At this point, she sees his brows knitting.

"Angus," she cries, "another penny for your thoughts!"

"Well, now," he frowns, "ma thoughts are more serious this time."

"Really?" whispers the girl, biting her lip in anticipation of the ultimate request.

"Aye," he says, "isn't it aboot time ye paid me them first three pennies?"

Why haven't women...

...been to the moon yet? It doesn't need cleaning.

At the barber's

A man walks into a barber's at lunchtime and asks how long it'll be before he can get his hair cut. The barber looks round at his shop full of hirsute customers and replies, "Two hours." The man leaves the shop.

Lunchtime the next day and he's back again, asking how long it'll be before he can get his hair cut. Once again the place is rammed, so the barber replies, "Two hours." The man walks out. The next day, same time, he's back for a third time, and once again the answer is two hours. He walks out – but this time the barber asks a friend to follow him and see where he goes. Twenty minutes pass and the friend returns, grim-faced. "Well," asks the barber, "where does he go?" "Your house."

The waiting game

A policeman is on night patrol near a local well-known Lovers' Lane, when he sees a car. The light is on and inside he can see a couple – a young man in the driver's seat reading a computer magazine, and a girl in the back seat calmly knitting. Suspicious, he wanders over to the driver's window and knocks. "Yes, officer?" says the young man, obligingly winding down the window, "can I help?"

"What do you think you're doing?" the policeman barks. "What does it look like?" answers the young man, "I'm reading this magazine." The copper points at the girl in the back seat. "And what is she doing?" he mutters. The young man glances over his shoulder. "I think," he says, "she's knitting a scarf." Confused, the officer asks, "How old are you, young man?"

"I'm 19," he replies. "And how old is she?" asks the officer, glancing at the young lady. The young man looks at his watch. "Well," he says after a thoughtful pause, "in about 12 minutes she'll be 16."

GIRLFRIEND? A: HE WIPED HIS ARSE.

What's the last thing...
...to go through a fly's head when it hits a windscreen?
Its arse.

Down boy

A man took his Rottweiler to the vet. "My dog's cross-eyed," he told the doc. "Is there anything you can do for him?"

"Well," said the vet, "let's see." So he picked the dog up by its ears and had a good look at its eyes. "Sorry," said the vet, "I'm going to have to put him down."

"Just because he's cross-eyed!" exclaimed the man. "No," said the vet. "Because he's bloody heavy."

Drunk takes a leak

A man is gently drinking himself into a stupor. After burping loudly, he turns groggily to the bartender. "Hey mate," he slurs, "where's your toilet?" With more than a little disdain, the bartender replies, "Go down the hall and it's on your right." Nodding dumbly, the man slides off his stool and stumbles off down the corridor. Within minutes, the other pub patrons jump at the sound of an ear-splitting scream. A few minutes of confusion go by, when suddenly another pained yell echoes around the bar. Locating the source of the noise, the barman decides to investigate, and runs into the pub toilets. "What's all the screaming about in here?" he shouts at the drunk. "You're scaring all my customers away."

"I'm sorry," he burbles, opening the cubicle door, "but I'm sitting on the toilet, and every time I go to flush it, something comes up and squeezes the hell out of my balls."

The bartender shakes his head sadly. "No wonder," he grimaces. "You're sitting on a mop bucket."

The engineer goes to Heaven

An engineer dies and reports to the Pearly Gates. Saint Peter checks his dossier and says, "Ah, I see you're an engineer – you're in the wrong place." So the engineer reports to the Gates of Hell and is let in. Pretty soon, however, the engineer gets dissatisfied with the level of comfort in Hell, and starts designing some improvements. Soon they've got air conditioning and flush toilets and

A horse walks into a bar...

...and asks for a pint. The barman thinks, "Hmm – I can rip off this horse without him realising," so charges £13 for the pint.

Serving the nag with his drink the barman says, "We don't get many horses in this pub."

"I'm not surprised," the horse replies, "the price you charge for a bloody pint."

Q: WHY SHOULD BLONDES NOT BE GIVEN COFFEE BREAKS?

escalators, and the engineer is a pretty popular guy. One day, God calls Satan up on the telephone and says with a sneer, "So, how's it going down there in Hell?"

"Hey, things are going great!" says the Devil. "We've got air conditioning and flush toilets and escalators! There's no telling what this engineer is going to come up with next…"

God replies, "What? You've got an engineer? That's a mistake – he should never have got down there. Send him back up."

"No way," says Satan. "I like having an engineer on the staff, and I'm keeping him."

"Send him back up here or I'll sue!" says God.

Satan laughs uproariously and answers, "Yeah, right. And just where are *you* going to get a lawyer?"

Codger orders ice-cream

Cedric and Bill, two old men suffering from Alzheimer's, are out walking one day when Cedric sees an ice-cream van at the end of a road. "Bill, go get me a 99," says Cedric, "a 99."

"I'll never remember that," replies Bill.

"Just think, '99, 99, 99,'" says Cedric.

So off trots Bill toward the ice-cream van, saying, "99, 99, 99," when Cedric calls him back. "Bill, get me some chopped nuts on that."

"Chopped whats on what?" replies poor Bill, looking confused.

"Just remember, '99, chopped nuts,'" says Cedric.

Again Bill wanders off, repeating Cedric's order over and over again. But no sooner has he walked a few steps when Cedric cries out, "Strawberry sauce as well!" Bill stops and turns around, "I'll never remember that."

"Look, Bill, remember 99, chopped nuts, strawberry sauce," Cedric patiently explains.

Off Bill wanders, saying, "99, nuts, strawberry sauce; 99, nuts, strawberry sauce; 99, nuts, strawberry sauce…"

Half an hour later, Bill comes back with a bag of chips.

"What do you call that!" shrieks Cedric.

"Bag of chips," says Bill.

"I can see that!" screams the other codger. "Where's my fucking pie!"

> **A bald cat…** …walks onto a bus in Liverpool and goes straight to the back. "Hey!" shouts the conductor. *"Where's your fur?"*

> **Did you hear about the man…** …who wouldn't pay for an exorcism? *He got re-possessed.*

Why don't fairies... ...get pregnant? *They only go to goblin parties.*

Redneck starts counting

After having their 11th child, a redneck couple decided that that was enough – they couldn't afford a larger trailer. So the husband went to his doctor (who also treated mules), and told him that he and his wife/cousin didn't want to have any more children. "Have you thought about a vasectomy?" asked the

The new monk feels randy

A man decides to join a monastery. On his first day he goes up to the abbot and says to him, "I know that we have to remain celibate, Father, but what happens when we feel the need to have sex?" The abbot replies, "Follow me," and leads him down to the cellar, where there's a large barrel with a hole in it. "Shove your penis in the hole whenever you need to satisfy your carnal urges," he explains. So the man tries it, and to his surprise enjoys it thoroughly.

"I can do this whenever I want?" he asks, scarcely believing his luck. "Why yes," says the abbot, "any day except Tuesday." The man asks him why. "Because it's your turn in the barrel," the abbot explains.

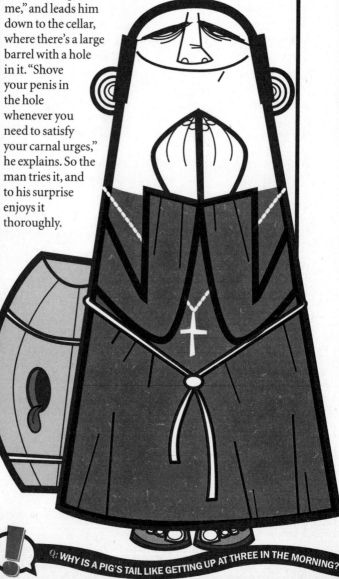

Q: WHY IS A PIG'S TAIL LIKE GETTING UP AT THREE IN THE MORNING?

doc. "Go home, get a banger, light it, put it in a beer can, then hold the can up to your ear and count to ten…"

"I may not be the smartest man in the world," said Cletus, "but I don't see how putting a banger in a beer can next to my ear is going to help me."

So the couple drove off to get a second opinion. "Go home, get a banger, light it, put it in a beer can, then hold the can up to your ear and count to ten…" said the second doc. Figuring that both learned physicians couldn't be wrong, the man went home, lit a banger and put it in a beer can. He held the can up to his ear and began to count: "One, two, three, four, five…" At this point he paused, placed the beer can between his legs, and picked up the count on his other hand…

The suspicious assistant

A man walks into a corner shop, looks around for a while and then goes up to the counter with a can of dog food. The man behind the counter says: "I'm sorry, I cannot sell you that tin of dog food."

"Why?!?"

"I've heard that you haven't got a dog, but that you eat the dog food yourself."

"That's a lie!"

"If you bring your dog in, I'll sell you the food," says the assistant.

The man leaves the shop in a huff, and returns later with his pet dog. The assistant duly sells him the dog food, and the man leaves.

The next day the man returns to buy a can of cat food. "I'm sorry – I cannot sell it to you," says the shop assistant.

"Why?!?"

"I've heard that you don't have a cat, but you've been eating the cat food yourself. If you bring your cat in, I will sell the food to you."

Again the man leaves the shop in a huff, returning with his pet cat. The shopkeeper duly sells him the food and he leaves.

The next day the man returns with a box under his arm, placing it on the table in front of the shopkeeper.

"What's this?" says the curious assistant.

"Put your hand in and you'll see…"

So the shopkeeper puts his hand in the box, then pulls it out. His hand is covered in shit. The man smiles and says, "A roll of toilet paper, please."

> **What's the difference…** …between a lamp and a hard-on? *You can sleep with a lamp on.*

> **A woman walks into a bar…** and asks for a double entendre. *So the barman gives her one.*

A: IT'S TWIRLY.

What's the difference... ...between a golf ball and a clitoris? A bloke will spend 15 minutes looking for a golf ball.

The dead cow

A farming family live off their only cow. One day, the mother wakes up to find that the cow has mysteriously died. Obviously distraught, she commits suicide, thinking that life is not worth living.

A few hours later, the father wakes up and finds his wife and cow dead. He also commits suicide.

The eldest son wakes up and sees that his parents are dead. But while he is trying to take his life in the lake, up pops a mermaid who says, "If you have sex with me five times in a row, I will make everything alright."

The son tries desperately, but only manages three times and commits suicide. Then the second eldest son wakes, to find that his brother and parents are dead. Off to the lake he goes…

Again the mermaid intervenes, "If you have sex with me ten times, I will make everything alright." The son tries, huffs and puffs, but dies from exhaustion after only seven shags.

Finally the youngest son wakes up, sees everyone dead, and attempts to commit suicide. The mermaid says, "If you have sex with me 15 times, I'll make everything alright." "Fifteen times?" says the youngest son. "You'll end up like the cow after I finish with you!"

The hungry rabbit

A rabbit is desperate for carrots, so he ventures into a butcher's shop for relief. "Got any carrots?" asks the bunny.

"No. Fuck off," says the butcher.

Undeterred, next day the rabbit tries his luck again. "Got any carrots?" he blurts.

"I've told you once and now I'm telling you again: no, I ain't got no carrots," says the evidently angry butcher. "You come in here again and I'll nail your ears to the floor – alright?"

"Okay, okay, no need to get hostile," says the rabbit, and hops out.

Next day, the floppy-eared one bounces into the shop again. "Got any nails?" says the bunny.

"No," says the butcher, perplexed.

"Good. Got any carrots?"

Never piss off a trucker

A trucker walked into a cafe and ordered a hamburger, a cup of tea and a jam doughnut. He had just sat down at a table and started reading his paper when three

What do you call an Australian... ...with a chip on both shoulders? Well balanced.

Q: WHY DON'T MEN LIKE WASHING MACHINES?

You shall go to the ball...

Cinderella goes to the ball, all kitted out by her fairy godmother, on one condition: that she return home by midnight or her fanny would turn into a watermelon. So off she trots, arriving at the ball only to be invited to sit and eat with the charming prince. The first course goes by, and the prince and Cinders are chatting away. The main meal goes by, and the prince and Cinders are laughing like drains. By the time they have to order their afters, the pair of them are flirting like mad. The prince has ordered watermelon, and he breaks off the chatter to tuck into the succulent fruit. He's loving it, chomping from side to side, juices going everywhere, all over his face and dribbling out the side of his mouth. Finally he turns to Cinderella and asks, "What time do you have to return home?" "4am," says Cinders.

Hell's Angels walked in. As they strode past his table, one shoved the burger in the trucker's face, the second drank his tea and the third one ate his doughnut. With that, the trucker stood up, paid his bill and left. One of the Hell's Angels turned to the waitress and said, "Huh! He ain't much of a man, is he?" To which the waitress replied: "He ain't much of a driver, either. He's just reversed over three motorcycles."

Good costume

A high-class fancy dress party is in full flow when suddenly a gorgeous blonde woman stalks in… completely nude. The alarmed host rushes to intercept her. "Where's your costume?" he hisses through clenched teeth.

"This is it," she explains. "I came as Adam."

"Adam?" her host explodes. "You don't even have a cock!"

"Oh, I don't know," she replies, "give me a few minutes."

The Halloween ball

A young couple were invited to a swanky masked Halloween party. On the night, the wife came down with a terrible headache, but she told her other half to go to the party anyway and have a good time. Being the devoted husband, he protested, but she argued and said she was going to take some aspirin and go to bed. So he put on his costume and away he went. The wife, after sleeping soundly for about an hour, awakened without pain, and as it was still early she decided to go to the party. And because hubby didn't know what her costume was, she thought she'd have some kicks watching her man to see how he acted when she was not around. So she joined the party, and soon spotted her husband cavorting around on the dancefloor. He was gettin' down with every bird he could, copping a feel here and taking a little kiss there. His wife sidled up to him; being a rather seductive babe herself, he left his partner high and dry and devoted his time to the new action. She let him go as far as he wished – he was her husband, after all. Finally he whispered a little proposition in her ear and, not a little turned on by the whole scenario, she agreed, so off they went to one of the cars and went at it like knives. Then, just before unmasking at midnight, she slipped out, went home, put the costume away and got

What's the difference... ...between muff-diving and driving in the fog? You can see the twat in front of you when you're muff-diving.

into bed, wondering what kind of excuse he would have for his outrageous behaviour. She was sitting up reading when he came in, and she asked him what he'd done. "Oh, the same old thing," he said. "You know I never have a good time when you're not there." Then she asked, "Did you dance much?" He replied, "I never even danced one dance. When I got to the party I met Pete,

Q: WHY WAS THE MAN ARRESTED FOR WAITING IN THE MARQUEE?

Bill and some other guys, so we went into the games room and played poker all evening. But I tell you – the bloke I loaned my costume to sure had one hell of a time."

The old lady's three wishes

An old lady is rocking away the last of her days on her front porch, reflecting on her long life, when all of a sudden her fairy godmother appears and informs her that she will be granted three wishes. "Well, now," says the old lady, "I guess I would like to be really rich."

Poof. Her rocking chair turns to solid gold.

"And, gee, I guess I wouldn't mind being a young, beautiful princess."

Poof. She turns into a beautiful young woman.

"Your third wish?" asks the fairy godmother. Just then the old woman's cat wanders across the porch in front of them. "Ooh – can you change him into a handsome prince?" she asks.

Poof. There before her stands a young man more handsome than anyone could possibly imagine. She stares at him, smitten. With a smile that makes her knees weak, he saunters across the porch and whispers in her ear, "I bet you're sorry you had me neutered…"

Just rewards

Little Johnny took his new chemistry set down to the cellar, where he stayed all afternoon mixing various liquids together. Eventually his dad went down and found him surrounded by test tubes, pounding something into the wall.

"Why are you hammering a nail into the wall?" asked dad. "It's not a nail," said Johnny. "It's a worm! I tried to bring this worm back to life with my special chemical mixture, but my formula made the worm hard as a rock."

Johnny showed his dad the liquid mix that he had soaked the worm in, and his dad said, "I'll tell you what. You give me the test tube with your special chemical mixture in it and I'll buy you a Toyota!"

So little Johnny handed the test tube over.

The next day, when Johnny got home from school, he saw a brand new Mercedes-Benz parked in the driveway. He then asked his dad about the car.

"Oh," said the father, "your Toyota is in the garage. The Mercedes is from your mother."

Peanut emergency

A man goes to his GP with a peanut stuck in his left ear. "What can I do to get it out?" he asks pathetically.

"Pour warm chocolate in the right ear and tilt your head," replies the doc.

"How the hell will that help?"

"Easy," replies the doc. "Next time you take a dump it'll come out a treat."

How can you tell…
…the difference between an Essex girl and an Essex boy? *The Essex girl has a higher sperm count.*

A: BECAUSE HE WAS LOITERING WITHIN TENT.

Silly name special

A young man called Hector Wankbreak worked for a company called "Big Ball, Small Ball Bavaria". He was in the works van when he got clocked doing 70mph in a 30 zone. A policeman pulled him over. "Can I have your name, please?" said the copper. Hector replied. Struggling not to laugh, the policeman wrote his name down. Then he asked what company Hector worked for. Stifling a giggle, the traffic cop wrote the details down. Then, with a warning, Hector was let off. However, it wasn't long before he was pulled over again. This new policeman also took amusement at Hector's name and business, and issued a strong warning. At the end of the day, the two policemen were writing up their reports and they saw that they had both bumped into Mr Wankbreak. They then decided to look in the phone book for Big Ball, Small Ball Bavaria – and sure enough, it was there. They proceeded to call up the number; when the phone was picked up, one of the officers said, "Hello there, I was wondering if you had a 'Wankbreak' there at all?" The reply was sharp. "You're joking, mate – we're lucky if we get a tea break."

> **Why are the Beatles...** ...like a blonde's knees? *Neither have been together since 1970.*

> **What does a blonde say...** ...to a bloke who has just blown in her ear? *Thanks for the refill.*

The drinking contest

A South African, an Aussie and a Cockney are sitting in a pub, drinking pints. The South African grabs his beer, downs it, throws his glass into the air, draws a handgun and shoots the glass in mid-air. Then he shouts, "In South Africa, we've got so many glasses we never drink out of the same glass twice." The Aussie then downs his beer, throws his glass into the air, grabs the gun off the bar, shoots the glass, puts the gun back on the bar and belches. "Mate, in Oz we have so many glasses, we too never drink out of the same pint-pot twice."
The Cockney looks at the two of them, finishes his beer, puts the glass down on the bar, picks up the gun and shoots both the Aussie and the South African. "In London," he says, "we've got so many South Africans and Aussies we never have to drink with the same ones twice."

The Presidents of Oz

Presidents Nixon, Bush and Clinton are travelling in a car in the American mid-west when a tornado whips up and whirls them into the air. When they come to, they realise they're in the Land of Oz, so they decide to go see the Wizard. Bush says, "I'm going

Q: DID YOU HEAR ABOUT THE MAN WHO FELL INTO AN

Finding the right word

Two sisters – one blonde, one brunette – inherit the family farm. Sadly, it's not long before financial trouble hits and, to keep the farm from being repossessed, they realise they must buy a bull and breed their own stock. With their last £1,000, the brunette heads to a farm where a prize bull is for sale. She tells her sister that, when she gets there, if she buys it she'll contact her so she can drive over with the trailer and take it home. The brunette arrives at the farm, inspects the creature and agrees to buy it. But there's a problem: the owner won't take a penny less than £999. Desperate, she pays up and drives in to town to send a telegram to her sibling. "I need a telegram to tell my sister I've bought a bull for our farm," explains the brunette. "She needs to hitch the trailer to our pickup, drive here and haul it home."

"No problem," the telegraph operator informs her, "but it's 99p per word."

With just one pound left, the brunette ponders which word could best explain her instructions. "Got it," she tells the old man. "Send the word 'comfortable'."

The telegraph operator shakes his head, "And how on Earth is that going to tell her what she needs to know?"

"My sister's blonde," explains the woman. "She'll read it very slowly…"

to ask the Wizard for a brain!" Nixon says, "I'm going to ask the Wizard for a heart!" Clinton says, "Where's Dorothy?"

Redneck humour

A young ventriloquist is touring the southern states of America and stops at a bar in South Carolina. He's going through his usual stupid redneck jokes when a big guy in the audience shouts, "I've heard just about enough of your smart-ass hillbilly jokes – we ain't all stupid here in the South." Flustered, the ventriloquist begins to apologise.

"You stay out of this, mister," roars the redneck. "I'm talking to the smart-ass little fella on your knee!"

UPHOLSTERY MACHINE? A: HE'S FULLY RECOVERED.

What's the difference...
...between a newly married man and an empty barrel of lager?
One has beery walls...

First day in the colony

Bob joins a very exclusive nudist colony. On his first day he takes off his clothes and starts wandering around. A gorgeous petite blonde walks by him and the man immediately gets an erection. The woman notices his erection, comes over to him grinning sweetly and says, "Sir, did you call for me?"

Bob replies, "No – what do you mean?"

"You must be new here," she says. "Let me explain. It's a rule here that if I give you an erection, it implies you called for me." Smiling, she then leads him to the side of a pool, lays down on a towel, eagerly pulls him to her and happily lets him have his way with her.

Bob continues exploring the facilities. He enters a sauna, sits down and farts. Within a few moments a huge, horribly corpulent, hairy man with a diamond-cutter erection lumbers out of the steam towards him. The huge man says, "Sir, did you call for me?"

Bob replies, "No – what do you mean?"

The huge man says, "You must be new here. It's a rule that when you fart, it implies you called for me." The huge man then easily spins Bob around, bends him over the bench and sodomises him. Bob rushes back to the colony office. He's greeted by the smiling naked receptionist, "May I help you?"

"Here's your card and key back," says Bob. "You can keep the £500 joining fee."

"But sir," says the receptionist. "You've only been here a couple of hours – you only saw a small part of our facilities..."

"Listen lady," Bob replies. "I'm 58 years old. I get a hard-on about once a month, but I fart 15 times a day. No thanks!"

Novelty scarf

A man with a 12-foot dick goes to visit the doctor. "I'm taking a girl out tonight," he explains. "It's my first ever date and I'm not sure what to do with my dick. Some people find it rather terrifying."

The doctor looks at the man pensively and finally advises him to paint it red, white and blue and hang it around his neck like a scarf. The man thanks the doctor for his advice and leaves to prepare for his hot date at the cinema.

Everything goes according to plan at the flicks, and the couple begin to get amorous... until half-way through the film the lights in the auditorium are switched on and a loud voice booms from the PA system, "Will the man with the red, white and blue scarf sitting on the back row, please stop flicking ice-cream over the other patrons."

Q: WHY DO HUSBANDS DIE BEFORE THEIR WIVES?

Kinky sex misunderstanding

A man walks into a bar and sits down next to a woman, who's drinking heavily. Plucking up courage he begins talking to the woman and asks why she's drinking like she is. The woman replies that she's depressed because her husband has left her – he's sick of her continual requests for kinky sex. The man thinks this is terrible and suggests the two of them have a lot in common, as his wife has just left him because of his repeated requests for kinky sex. One thing leads to another and, drunk, they end up leaving the bar together. They go back to the woman's house, where she tells the man to make himself comfortable while she slips into something more sexy.

She goes into her bedroom and puts on her kinky sex gear, then bursts back out into the living room.

The man, however, is in the process of putting his coat on and is about to leave.

"Where are you going?" she enquires. "I thought we were going to have kinky sex together?"

"Too late," the man replies. "I've already screwed your dog and crapped in your purse. I'm out of here!"

How do you turn a duck... ...into a soul singer? Put it in the microwave until it's Bill Withers.

Toast therapy

A husband and wife notice that their little boy's penis is a little too small, so they take him to the doctor. The quack says to feed the little boy lots of toast, so the next morning, the wife gets up really early and makes a huge stack of toast.

"Take the top two slices," the mother tells the little boy when he comes down to breakfast. "The rest are for your father."

Drinker rebuffed

A man is drinking alone at the bar when two stunning young females walk in. The man calls the barman over and asks him what the girls are drinking, then buys them each a G&T. Twice more he sends the drinks over, this without as much as a glance from the girls.

The third time, he tells the barman to get them doubles. Finally, to his excitement, one of the girls slinks towards him and whispers in his ear, "Would you like to smell my friend's pussy?"

"Well, yes I would!" replies the man. And the girl exhales in his face.

A: THEY WANT TO. THEY JUST WANT TO.

A bloke walks into...

...work one day and says to a colleague, "Do you like my new shirt – it's made out of the finest silk and got loads of cactuses over it."
"Cacti," says the co-worker.
"Forget my tie," says the bloke. "Look at my shirt!"

Dinner party disaster

A wife and her husband are throwing a dinner party for some important French guests. At the last minute, disaster strikes – they've forgotten the snails! "Take a bucket, run to the beach and get some," says the man's wife. He agrees and off he goes.

As he's collecting the slippery critters, he spies a stunning woman strolling alongside the water a little further down the beach. "Imagine… if she would even just come over and talk to me, I'd be in Heaven…" he thinks to himself.

All of a sudden, he notices the gorgeous young woman is standing right over him. They begin talking, she soon invites him back to her place and they embark on a night of filth and debauchery. At dawn, the man wakes up, "Oh shit! The dinner party!" He pulls on his clothes, grabs his bucket of snails and runs out the door. He belts it all the way home, but as he's running up the house steps, he trips and the snails end up all over the place. The door opens – his wife is fuming. Quick as a flash he looks down at the scattered snails, "Come on fellas! We're almost there!"

Rhino horniness

A man is having trouble in the "bedroom department" – a severe case of brewer's droop. His wife threatens to leave him, so in desperation he promises to try a new type of Chinese medicine. He goes to the local acupuncture clinic and asks for the strongest aphrodisiac they have, and they give him a large jar filled with powder. "What is it?" he asks. "Powdered rhino horn," he's told.

So he goes home and tells the wife. She's happy that he's taken action to address the problem and says, "You take the potion and I'll go upstairs and wait for you." She's already slipped upstairs when he realises there are no instructions, so he downs the whole jar, then he goes up to the bedroom. His wife is lying there in her bra and panties. "Go ahead and do what you want," she purrs. So he runs up the neighbour's drive and butts their Range Rover.

Do you know why the blonde got fired...

...from the M&M factory? *She kept throwing out all the Ws.*

Q: WHAT'S GREY AND HIDES BEHIND BUSHES?

The genie's dilemma

A man's having a quiet pint at his local when a drunk staggers past, dropping a gold key-ring. Before the man can say anything, the drunk's disappeared out the door, so he picks up the key-ring from the beer-soaked floor and gives it a wipe on his sleeve. To the man's surprise a genie appears! "Right, lad – you know the crack," says the genie. "You get one wish for setting me free."
The man ponders for a minute. "I'm a big fan of motor racing, but the travel's a drag," he says. "Can I have a major motorway route linking all the circuits in England?" "Nay, sonny," says the fearsome figure. "Do you know how many men I'll have to take on to do that? All the materials and overheads? The logistics would be a nightmare. There must be something else you could wish for…"
The man thinks long and hard, then replies, "Okay, smart-arse, I want you to tell me how a woman's mind works."
"How many lanes do you want?"

A: A CAR PARK.

> # What's the biggest drawback... ...in the circus? *An elephant's foreskin.*

Mountie misunderstanding

An eccentric English colonel met a Canadian Mountie in a bar and expressed an interest in joining Canada's finest. The Mountie explained that there was a traditional initiation ceremony and invited the colonel over to Vancouver the following week.

Once there, the Mounties explained that the initiation involved drinking a whole bottle of Canadian Club whisky, then venturing into the nearby forest to shoot a grizzly bear, before finishing off by making love to an Inuit girl.

The Colonel accepted and, after downing the bottle of Canadian Club, he staggered off in the direction of the forest. An hour later he returned, his clothes torn, battered and bruised and covered in blood.

"Okay," he said, "where's this Inuit girl I've got to shoot?"

One-upmanship

Four businessmen are playing golf. At the first hole, the first man says, "I'm so important that my company has bought me this nuclear-powered mobile phone so I can keep in touch all over the world."

At the second hole, the next man says, "I'm so important to my company that they have sewn my mobile phone to the palm of my hand."

At the third hole, the third man starts mumbling away to himself. "Who are you talking to?" ask the other three, to which he replies, "I'm so important to my company that they've inserted a miniature mobile phone in my lip."

They get to the next hole, when all of a sudden the fourth man makes a dash for the bushes. The others wait for ten minutes before going to check if he's alright. They peep through the bushes and find him squatting with his trousers around his ankles. "Oh, sorry," they apologise. "It's okay," the fourth man replies, "I'm just expecting a fax."

Prankster not amused

Paul Daniels is doing tricks on live TV, but he runs out of "magic" with five minutes to go, so he asks if anyone in the audience has any tricks. A guy puts his hand up and Paul invites him onto the stage. Paul then asks him what he needs for the trick. The bloke replies, "Your assistant – the lovely Debbie – and a table." Paul is slightly confused but gets the table and Debbie anyway. The guy then bends Debbie over the table and starts rodding her from behind. Paul, slightly concerned about the situation, says, "What are you doing? This isn't a trick." "I know," replies the bloke, "but it's fucking magic."

> # What's green... ...and eats balls? *Gonorrhoea.*

The sergeant's staff

A sergeant major stomps into a brothel, "I am here for a woman!" he shouts. He is immediately escorted upstairs to the best girl, where he disrobes and booms, "Woman, I've been in the army 30 years and I'm a master of my mind and body! DICK! 'TEN-HUT!'" Immediately, his penis is fully erect.

"Sweet mama! How did you do that?" asks the prostitute.

"Been in the army 30 years," shouts the sarge, "and I'm a master of my mind and body! DICK! AT EASE!" And with that, his penis goes limp. The prostitute is amazed and requests another demonstration.

"Wilco," he hollers, "been in the army 30 years and I'm a master of my mind and body! DICK! 'TEN-HUT!'"

Again, his cock stands proud. "DICK! AT EASE!" he booms, but when he glances down, he's still hard as a rock. "Apparently you didn't HEAR me soldier! DICK! AT EASE!"

Still nothing happens. "I'm giving you one last chance," he fumes, "DICK! AT EASE!"

But nothing happens, so he grabs his penis and starts tugging furiously. "What the Hell's going on?" asks the prostitute. "Stand back, ma'am!" he shouts. "For disobeying a direct order, this soldier's getting a dishonourable discharge!"

Satan gets stumped

One beautiful Sunday morning, the tiny town of Smithvale wakes up and goes to church. Before the service starts, most of the congregation have seated themselves. They're all nattering to their neighbours when – shazam! – Satan himself appears at the altar in a flash of flame. Naturally the church erupts in chaos, with people fleeing left, right and centre – except for Bill Scroggs. Beelzebub is confused. He walks up to Bill and says, "Don't you know who I am?"

Bill replies, "Aye, I do."

Bewildered, Satan asks, "So you aren't afraid of me, then?"

"No I'm not," says Bill calmly.

By now, Satan's melon is twisted beyond all recognition. "Why the hell not?" the Dark Overlord enquires.

"Because I've been married to your sister for 25 years," Bill replies.

Blighted by verse

Tony Blair is being shown around a hospital. Towards the end of his visit, he strolls into a ward whose patients appear to have no obvious sign of injury. He greets the first patient and the chap replies, "Fair fa' your honest, sonsie face, Great chieftain o' the puddin-race! Aboon them a' ye tak your place, Painch, tripe, or thairm: Weel are ye wordy of a grace, As lang's my arm."

Baffled, Tony simply effects his usual big stupid grin and moves on to the next patient, who instantly pipes up, "Wee, sleekit, cowrin',

Q: WHAT'S WHITE AND FLUFFY AND LIVES IN TREES?

tim'rous beastie, O, what a panic's in thy breastie! Thou need na start awa sae hasty, Wi' bickering brattle! I wad be laith to rin an' chase thee, Wi' murd'ring pattle!"

Tony turns to the doctor. "Forgive me, are we in the mental ward?" he asks.

"No," replies the doctor, "Burns unit."

How old am I?

An old man took pride in his appearance, and didn't look anywhere near his actual age of 74. He walked into a pub one afternoon and ordered a pint. When the barman gave the man his pint, the old man said, "Guess how old I am!" The barman thought for a while and said, "50?" The old man laughed. "I'm 74," he said proudly.

"Surely not," said the barman, "you don't look a day over 50."

Feeling extremely happy the man drank his pint and wandered off towards the chemist. In the chemist, he did the same thing. "Tell me," he said to the woman behind the counter, "how old do you think I am?" The woman thought, and said eventually, "50?"

"No!" laughed the man. "I'm 74!"

"Wow!" exclaimed the woman. "You look great." The man paid for his goods and left. Later, while he was standing at the bus stop, an old woman approached and stood next to him.

> # What does a blonde's... ...right leg say to her left leg? *Nothing – they've never met.*

"Tell me," he said again. "How old do you think I am?"

"Oh, I'm good at these games," said the woman. "But what you'll have to do is get your willy out." The man looked around, and couldn't see anyone else, so he pulled down his trousers and got his willy out. The woman grabbed it and began to rub. This went on for about five minutes until she said, "Right – now let me guess." She pondered for a while, then said, "74!" Amazed, the man questioned her, "How on Earth did you know that?"

"I was standing behind you in the chemist's," she said.

Fairy developments

Snow White walks into her local chemist to pick up some photos she left for developing. Sadly, due to a technical glitch, the assistant informs her that her photos have been delayed, and that he's unable to give her a time when she can pick them up. With a look of despair, Snow White bursts into song, "Some day my prints will come..."

A MERINGUE-UTAN.

The two hikers

After hiking through the woods for hours, two women come to a stream. Unable to cross, they decide to look for a narrower part – and soon they come across an old bridge spanning the water. Deciding that the bridge is safe, the two women proceed to walk over it. Halfway across, one woman stops. "You know," she says, "I've always wanted to be like a bloke and piss off a bridge."

"Well I don't see anyone around," replies her friend. "Now's your chance."

So the first woman pulls down her hiking shorts and backs over to the side of the bridge. But just as she begins to urinate, she looks over her shoulder.

"Holy shit!" she exclaims, "I just pissed on a canoe!" Alarmed, the second woman peeks at the stream. "That wasn't a canoe," she says. "That was your reflection."

The Good Samaritan

Bob goes into the public restroom and sees a man standing next to the urinal. The man has no arms. As Bob's standing there, taking care of business, he wonders to himself how the poor wretch is going to take a leak. Bob finishes and starts to leave when the man asks Bob to help him out. Being a kind soul, Bob says, "Okay, sure."

"Can you unzip my zipper?" asks the man.

"Okay," says Bob.

"Can you pull it out for me?" asks the man.

"Uh, yeah, okay," says Bob. So he pulls it out. It's covered in all kinds of mould and bumps, with hair clumps, rashes, moles, scabs and scars, and it reeks something awful. Then the guy asks Bob to point it for him, and Bob points it for him. Bob then shakes it, puts it back in and zips up the man's flies for him.

"Thanks, I really appreciate it," the man tells Bob.

"No problem," says Bob, "I hope you don't mind me asking, but what's wrong with your penis?"

The guy pulls his arms out of his shirt. "I don't know," he says, "but I sure as hell ain't touching it."

> **Police arrested two kids yesterday... ...one was drinking battery acid, the other was eating fireworks. They charged one and let the other one off.**

Wild West medicine

There were two church-going women gossiping in front of a store when a cowboy rode up. He tied up in front of the saloon, walked around behind his horse and slapped his mouth full on its rectum.

One of the stunned women cried, "That's disgusting, why did you do that?"

"I've got chapped lips," replied the cowpoke.

Confused, the woman continued, "Does that make them feel better?"

"No," said the cowboy, "but it sure as hell stops me from licking them."

Q: WHY COULDN'T DRACULA'S WIFE GET TO SLEEP?

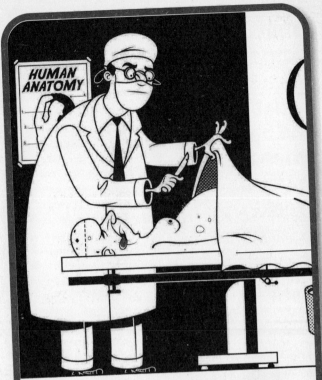

The dead man's dick

A coroner is working late at the hospital, and as he's preparing Mr Smith for the crematorium he makes an amazing discovery: Smith had the longest cock he's ever seen. After surveying it in awe for a few minutes, the man comes to a decision. "I'm sorry Mr Smith," he says to the corpse, "but I can't send you off to be cremated with such a tremendous cock." And with that, the coroner takes his scalpel and quickly removes the dead man's spam javelin.

Rushing over to the genito-urinary department, he asks his surgeon pal to perform a penis transplant on him. Upon waking from the operation, the coroner stuffs his tuberous prize into his briefs and goes home. His wife opens the door, and immediately asks where he's been. "Honey! Don't worry!" he says, opening his fly, "I have something wonderful to show you."

"Oh my God!" she screams, "Smith's dead!"

A: BECAUSE OF HIS COFFIN.

What do women get... ...that's long and hard when they marry a Greek? A surname.

Camel talk

A mother and baby camel are talking one day when the baby camel asks, "Mum – why have I got these huge three-toed feet?"

The mother replies, "Well, son, when we trek across the desert your toes will help you to stay on top of the soft sand."

"Okay," says the lad. A few minutes later the son asks, "Mum, why have I got these great long eyelashes?"

"They're there to keep the sand out of your eyes on the trips through the desert."

"Thanks, Mom," replies the li'l camel.

After a short while, the son returns and asks, "Mum, why have I got these great big humps on my back?"

The mother, now a little impatient with the boy, replies, "They're there to help us store water for our long treks across the desert, so we can go without drinking for long periods."

"That's great, Mum," says the baby camel, thinking for a minute. "So what are we doing in Whipsnade?"

Infidelity explained

A woman arrives home after a shopping trip, walks into the bedroom and is horrified to find her husband going at it hammer and tongs with a young, attractive female.

Just as she's set to storm out of the house, her husband leaps up, "Before you leave, I want you to hear how this all came about. Driving home, I saw this young girl, poor and tired, so I offered her a ride. She was starving, so I brought her home and fed her some of the roast you'd forgotten about in the refrigerator. Her shoes were falling apart, so I gave her a pair of yours you no longer wear because they're out of style. She was freezing, so I gave her that new birthday sweater you've never worn because 'the colour doesn't suit you'. Her trousers were threadbare, so I gave her a pair of yours that no longer fit you. Then, just as she was leaving, she paused and asked, 'Is there anything else your wife doesn't use any more?' And so here we are…"

Dinner's ready!

A sex-starved housewife decided she'd gone without for too long, so she stripped naked and waited upstairs for her husband to return. As soon as he shut the door behind him, she came out of hiding and slid down the banister. Shocked, her husband asked, "What are you doing, woman?"

To which she replied, "Warming up your dinner."

Dissatisfied customer

A woman walked into a sex shop and asked for a vibrator. The shop assistant gestured with his index finger and said, "Come this way." The woman replied, "If I could come that way, I wouldn't need a bloody vibrator."

Q: HOW DO YOU BLIND A WOMAN?

Mice in love

There were two mice named Josephine and Earnest. They were in love and used to visit one another every day to have a coffee. They lived a long way apart so it was a big trek every afternoon. One day it was Josephine's turn to visit Earnest, and she was merrily trotting along, humming a little song to herself. She was running a little late so she decided to use the shortcut across the field. She was a little way in when she heard a faint noise in the distance.

She paused and listened. "Whirrrrrrr chunka chunka whirrrrrrrr chunka chunka."

The noise was getting progressively louder. She thought to herself, "That's strange…" and she continued on her way, a bit faster this time.

Before long the noise was overbearing. The ground started to vibrate. She stopped running and looked around just in time to see sharp blades coming down on top of her. She screamed, but her screams were lost in the piercing noise. She was picked up, tossed around, scraped, cut and beaten, until she was just a quivering pulp. Only then was it over.

She crawled bleeding to Earnest's house and dragged herself to the door. Earnest rushed out and held her in his arms. "Darling," said her mouse lover. "What happened to you?"

"Earnest," she whispered, "it was awful. I've been reaped."

Tall tale

Two hobbits walk into a bar where one of them picks up a woman. They take her to a local motel; the first hobbit goes into the motel room while the other waits outside. Once the door closes, the hobbit on the outside hears strange noises through the door, "I can't do it, I can't do it, I CAN'T DO IT!"

In the morning, the second hobbit asks the first, "How did it go?"

The first one answers, "It was embarrassing. I simply couldn't do it."

The second hobbit shakes his head, "Manhood problems, eh?"

"No. I couldn't get on the bed!"

Why is pubic hair… …curly?

If it were straight it would poke your eyes out.

Three strikes you're out

A farmer just got married and was going home on his wagon pulled by a team of horses. When one of the horses stumbled, he said, "That's once."

Then it stumbled again. He said, "That's twice."

Later, it stumbled a third time. This time, he didn't say anything, just pulled out a shotgun and shot the horse dead.

His wife cried out and started to yell at him. The farmer turned to her and said, "That's once."

The bus driver and the baby

A woman got on a bus, holding a baby. "Hot damn!" exclaimed the driver. "That's the ugliest baby I've *ever* seen!" In a huff, the woman slammed her fare down and tramped to the rear of the bus, where she sat, fuming.

The man seated next to her sensed she was agitated and asked what was wrong.

"The bus driver insulted me!" explained the woman.

The man sympathised. "He's a public servant," he said. "He shouldn't say things to insult the passengers."

"You're right!" said the woman. "I think I'll go back up there and give him a piece of my mind!"

"That's a good idea," the man said. "Let me hold your monkey."

Q: HOW DO YOU MAKE YOUR WIFE CRY WHILE HAVING SEX?

No betting man

A chap walks into a butcher's and asks for a pound of mince. "No problem, mate," says the butcher. "In fact I will give you £1,000 if you can reach the meat hanging above your head."
"A thousand pounds, you say…" The guy thinks about it then says, "Sorry, I'm not even going to try."
"Why the hell not? This is a great offer!" says the butcher.
"Sorry Mr Butcher, but the steaks are just too high."

Complimentary check-up

A middle-aged woman is at home, merrily jumping up and down on her bed and squealing with delight. Her husband arrives home from work, walks in and is astounded at what he sees. "Do you have any idea how ridiculous you look?" he shouts. "What the hell's the matter with you?"
"I just came from the doctor," replies his wife. "He says I have the breasts of an 18-year-old!"
"Oh really," says her husband, "and what did the old coot say about your 40-year-old arse?"
"Strangely enough," replies his wife, "your name never came up…"

Paging Dr Freud

A man goes to a psychiatrist. "Doc," he says, "I keep having these alternating recurring dreams. First I'm a marquee; then I'm a wigwam; then I'm a marquee; then I'm a wigwam again. It's driving me crazy. What's wrong with me?"
"It's very simple," the doctor replies. "You're two tents."

The crossword fanatics

Two blokes are sitting in a pub having a pint. One of them is doing the crossword. "Eight letters," he reads out, "centre of female pleasure."
"Clitoris," says the other.
"Do you know how to spell that?" asks the crossword fan.
"No," replies the other. "You should have asked me last night – it was on the tip of my tongue."

Bad reception

A blonde went to an electronics store and asked, "How much is this TV?" The salesman said, "Sorry, we don't sell to blondes." The next day she came back as a brunette. She asked the salesman how much the TV was. He said, "Sorry, we don't sell to blondes." The next day she came back as a redhead and asked the salesman how much the TV was. He said, "Sorry we don't sell to blondes." She replied, "I came in here as a brunette and a redhead. How do you know I am a blonde?" "Because that is not a TV, it's a microwave."

Pre-paid plan

A guy goes to a brothel. He selects a girl, pays her £200 up front and gets undressed. She's about to take off her sheer blue negligée, when the fire alarm rings. She runs out of the room, with his £200 still in her hand. He quickly grabs his clothes and runs out after her. He's searching the building, but the smoke gets too heavy, so he runs outside looking for her. By this time, the firemen are there. He sees one of them and asks, "Did you see a beautiful blonde, in a sheer blue negligée, with £200 in her hand?" The fireman says, "No!" The guy then says, "Well if you see her, screw her. It's paid for."

PHONE HER UP.

Proud father

A man has six children and is very proud of his achievement. He is so proud of himself that he starts calling his wife "Mother of Six" in spite of her objections.

One night they go to a party. The man decides that it's time to go home, and wants to find out if his wife is ready to leave as well.

He shouts at the top of his voice, "Shall we go home now Mother of Six?"

His wife, finally fed up with her husband, shouts back, "Any time you're ready, Father of Four!"

A materialist lawyer?

There was a lawyer who drove his shiny new Merc to work one day. He parked it in front of the company where he worked to show it off to all his lawyer colleagues. As he got out, a lorry hit the door and ripped it right off. The driver stopped and ran to the lawyer saying "Are you alright, are you alright?"

The lawyer, now furious, started to scream and berate the driver. "What the hell do you think you are doing? This is my brand new Mercedes… You know, I am a lawyer and I am going to sue you for all you are worth!"

Then a policeman ran up to the scene and said to the lawyer, "Calm down! You lawyers are so materialistic it's disgusting! Don't you know, when that lorry ripped your door off, it took your arm with it?"

The lawyer looked down and saw his left arm missing and said, "Oh God… my Rolex!"

Sex gift

Adam was talking to his friend at the bar, and he said, "I don't know what to get my wife for her birthday – she has everything, and besides, she can afford to buy anything she wants, so I'm stuck."

His friend said, "I have an idea! Why don't you make up a certificate saying she can have 60 minutes of great sex, any way she wants it. She'll probably be thrilled." Adam decided to take his friend's advice.

The next day at the bar his friend said, "Well? Did you take my suggestion?"

"Yes, I did," Adam replied.

"Did she like it?"

"Oh yes! She jumped up, thanked me, kissed me on the forehead and ran out the door, yelling, 'I'll be back in an hour!'"

My what a lovely cucumber

A beautiful woman loved to garden, but couldn't seem to get her tomatoes to turn red. One day while taking a stroll she came upon a neighbour who had the most beautiful garden full of huge red tomatoes.

The woman asked the gentleman, "What do you do to get your tomatoes red?"

The gentleman responded, "Well, twice a day I stand in front of my tomato garden and expose myself, and my tomatoes turn red from blushing so much."

The woman was so impressed, she decided to try doing the same thing to her tomato garden to see if it would work. So twice a day for two weeks she exposed herself to her garden hoping for the best.

One day the gentleman was passing by and asked the woman, "By the way, how did you make out? Did your tomatoes turn red?"

"No," she replied, "but my cucumbers are enormous."

The squaddie's bonus

Upon returning from the Falklands War, General Thompson calls his three toughest fighters to his office for a debrief. "Gentlemen, I want you to know your efforts were appreciated," the General begins. "So the top brass have decided to let each of you choose two parts of your body to be measured, then be given £100 for each inch between those points. Fair?"

The men nod slowly – before the first, a Commando, steps up. "Sah!" he shouts, "I choose the top of me head to me toes, sah!" Nodding, the General pulls out his tape measure. "Very good," he barks. "That's 70 inches… which comes to £7,000."

An expert sniper is next up. "Sah! I'm going for the tip of one hand to the other, sah!" he shouts. "Even better," replies the General, measuring his outstretched arms. "That's 72 inches, which comes to £7,200."

Finally, an explosives expert in the infantry steps forward. "Sah!" he shouts, "I'll go for the tip of my dick to my balls, sah!"

The General frowns. "That's a strange request, soldier," he mutters, "but drop your trousers." He bends down, tape measure in hand, but quickly stands up again. "My God, soldier!" he cries. "Where are your balls?"

The soldier smiles. "Falkland Islands, sah."